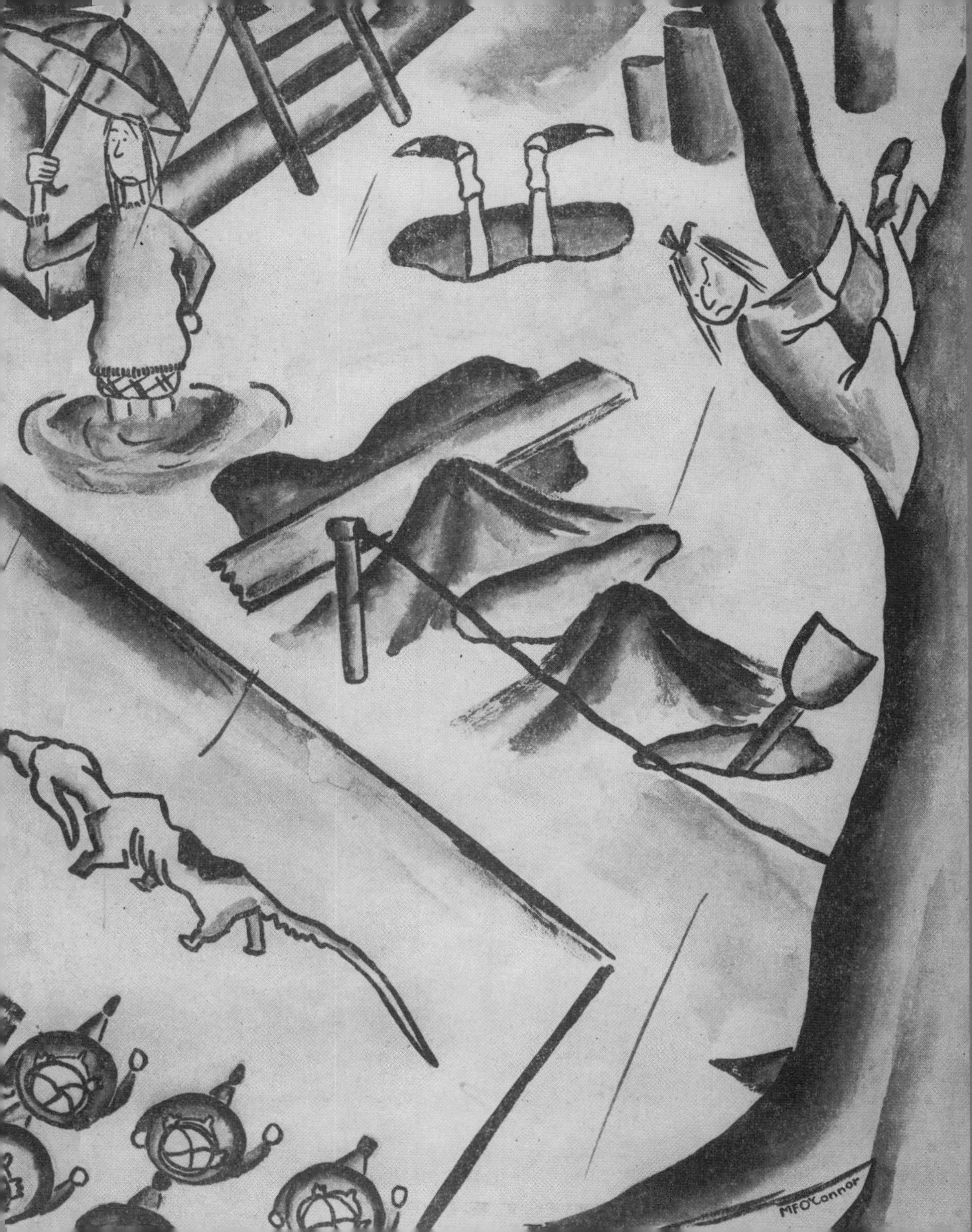
MFO'Connor

FLANNERY O'CONNOR

THE CARTOONS

Fantagraphics Books
7563 Lake City Way NE
Seattle, Washington 98115

Editor: KELLY GERALD
Editorial Liaisons: GARY GROTH and JASON T. MILES
Designer: JACOB COVEY
Associate Publisher: ERIC REYNOLDS
Publishers: GARY GROTH and KIM THOMPSON

All photographs of Flannery O'Connor and of campus scenes from Georgia State College for Women
are provided by the Flannery O'Connor Collection, Georgia College and State University Library,
Milledgeville, Georgia.

The captions for Flannery O'Connor's cartoons, as they originally appeared in her high school and
college's student publications, included irregular capitalization and punctuation that do not reflect a
clear artistic intention. The presentation of her captions is standardized for this publication, following
the prevailing trends evident among her cartoons.

Thanks to Ben Camardi for his enthusiasm, professionalism, and confidence.

To receive a free full-color catalog of comics, graphic novels, prose novels, artist monographs, and
other fine works of high artistry, call 1-800-657-1100, or visit www.fantagraphics.com. You may order
books at our website or by phone.

Distributed in the U.S. by W.W. Norton and Company, Inc. (800-233-4830)
Distributed in Canada by Canadian Manda Group (800-452-6642 x862)
Distributed in the U.K. by Turnaround Distribution (44 (0)20 8829-3002)
Distributed to comic stores by Diamond Comics Distributors (800-452-6642 x215)

ISBN: 978-1-60699-479-5
First Fantagraphics Books printing: April, 2012
Printed by Imago

FLANNERY O'CONNOR

THE CARTOONS

EDITED by KELLY GERALD

with an introduction by Barry Moser

FANTAGRAPHICS BOOKS

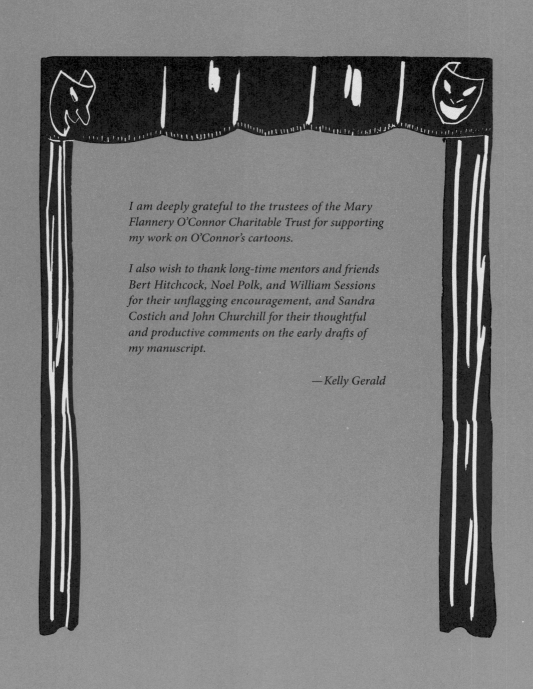

I am deeply grateful to the trustees of the Mary Flannery O'Connor Charitable Trust for supporting my work on O'Connor's cartoons.

I also wish to thank long-time mentors and friends Bert Hitchcock, Noel Polk, and William Sessions for their unflagging encouragement, and Sandra Costich and John Churchill for their thoughtful and productive comments on the early drafts of my manuscript.

—Kelly Gerald

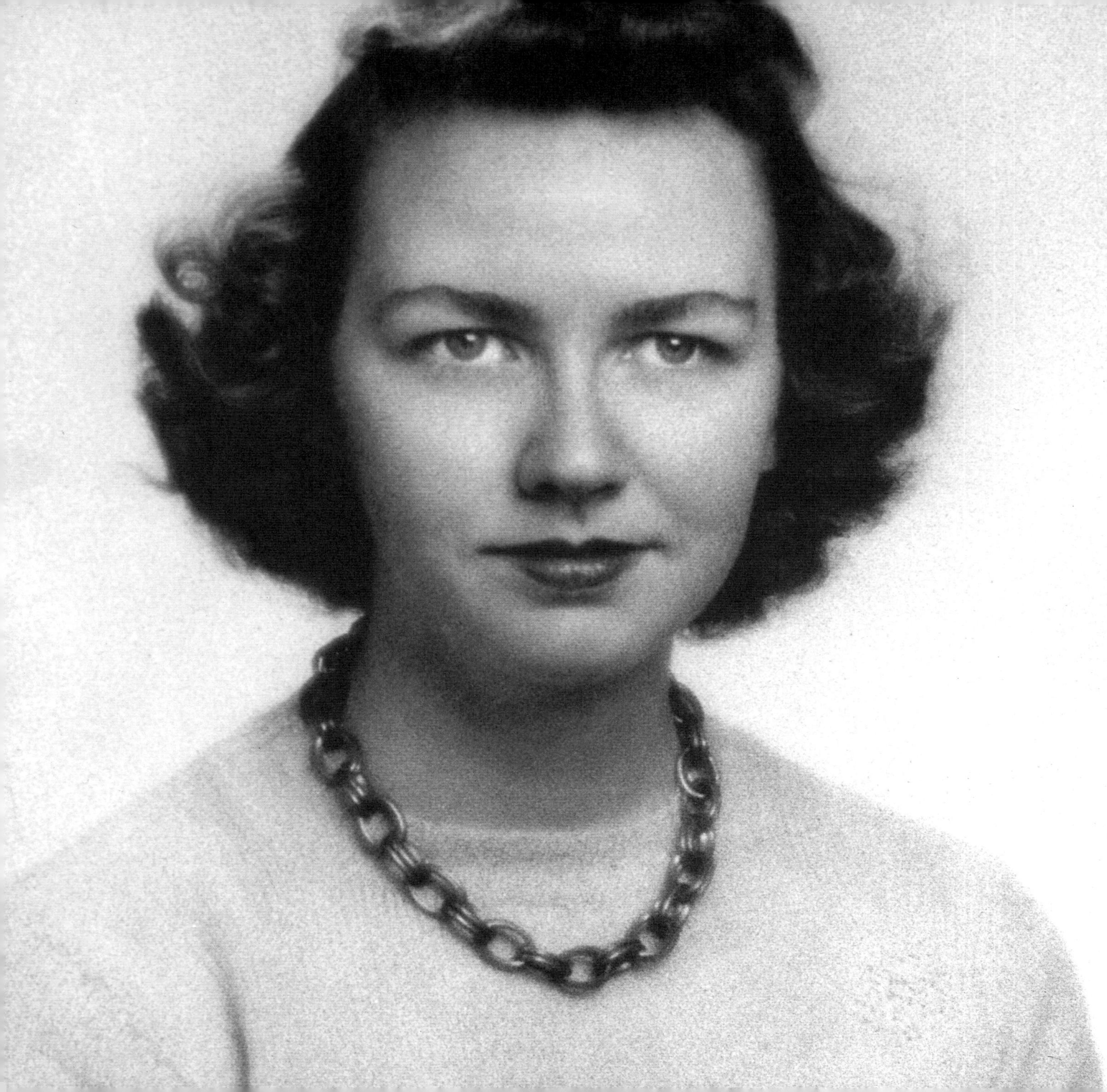

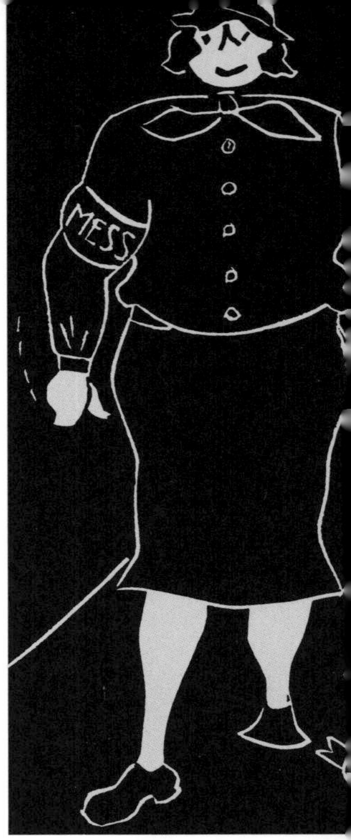
MESS

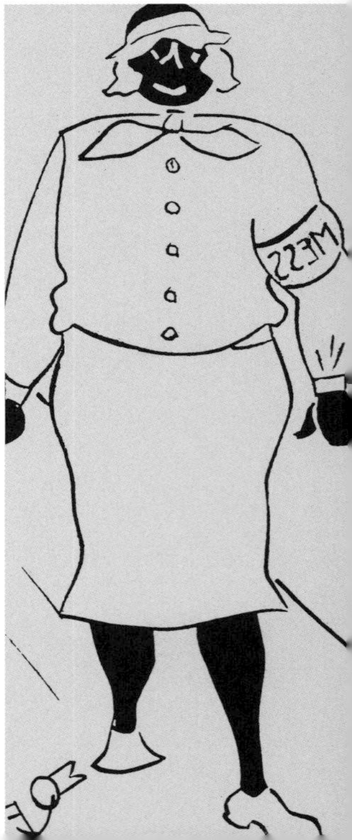

WORKING BACKWARD

A REFLECTION ON THE LINOLEUM CUTS OF FLANNERY O'CONNOR BY BARRY MOSER

Flannery O'Connor kept a pet chicken when she was a small child and trained it to walk backward — it was the subject of a 1931 Pathé film "short," a brief human interest story that came between the Pathé news and the feature picture show. The five-year-old Flannery was in the picture "to assist the chicken," but later said that it was "the high point" in her life, adding, "Everything since has been anticlimax."[1]

When I saw the film at Georgia College a few years ago I laughed out loud because it was, it seemed to me, a harbinger of the droll, baroque fiction that O'Connor would begin writing years later, never mind her lifelong love affair with domestic fowl of all sorts, especially chickens and peafowl.

So, when I began studying her linoleum cuts, that short film came back to me. It came back for the simple reason that linoleum cuts are drawn and cut backward. This is a categorical fact of all printmaking media, except offset lithography: The image, as cut, engraved, or etched on the plate or block is reversed left and right when it is printed. There's no way around it. It's always been that way. Always will be.

Some printmaking media tend toward exorbitant degrees of complexity, precision, chemistry, and sophistication: Stone lithography, mezzotints, and viscosity prints are examples. Other printmaking media, such as linoleum cuts and woodcuts, are generally lacking such precision and complexity, unless, of course, we talk about the woodcuts of artists like Fritz Eichenberg or Albrecht Dürer and his crowd, who cut their images into very, very hard wood with very, very sharp tools.

The potato print, which is made by cutting into the flat face of a halved potato, removing lines and shapes using whatever simple tools are at hand — say, a teaspoon or table knife — then rolling ink onto the surface and stamping it on paper, is probably the most elemental printmaking technique there is. Thus it is a favorite with elementary school art classes. The linoleum cut is a few notches above the potato print in difficulty and durability, but it is still, by far, the simplest, easiest, and crudest of all the printmaking media — save, of course, the above-mentioned potato print. Whatever is cut away receives no ink, and thus those areas print as white lines or shapes. Nothing could be more direct or fundamental. (Given O'Connor's sense of humor and her penchant for the absurd, I wonder if she ever thought about using potatoes instead of linoleum?

OPPOSITE: O'Connor before she graduated from Georgia State College for Women in 1945.

Had she, it would have added an element of subtle tomfoolery, a characteristic she was, I think it safe to say, never beyond.)

printmaking media are classified as either fine or broad. (They are also classified in terms of the surface from which they are pulled: relief, intaglio, or planographic. But to make these technical distinctions here is far beyond the scope of this introduction. The curious reader can find scores of books on the subject, both general and specific.)

Fine printmaking media are intricate, sophisticated, precise, and often highly technical in their nature. Etchings and engravings (both intaglio and relief), typically, are fine media.

Broad printmaking media tend more toward being bold and unrefined. Linoleum cuts and woodcuts are broad media. Woodcuts can, in the hands of a master, as mentioned above, rise to the level of being a fine medium. But very few printmakers have ever succeeded in making linoleum cuts into a fine medium.[2]

Flannery O'Connor's prints are good examples of the broad nature of the medium. Cut in what appears to be raw haste, her prints are naïve in their craftsmanship. But so what? One does not really expect accomplished, sophisticated art from a college student, much less in a college newspaper, and in this O'Connor is not an exception.

Her cuts are coarse in technical terms. I suspect that most of them were done inside an hour's time. If not, then she was dawdlin.' This is very much in keeping with the medium. When worked warm, as on a hot plate, linoleum cuts like butter. The cutting tools meet little, if any, resistance. It cuts quick and easy. Later in her life she would say the things she worked on the hardest were usually her worst work.[3] It is obvious she did not work long and hard on these images, and that is very much a part of their charm. She also said that a story — or a linoleum print, if you will — has to have muscle as well as meaning, and the meaning has to be in the muscle.[4] Her prints certainly have muscle, and a lot of it.

Her rudimentary handling of the medium notwithstanding, O'Connor's prints offer glimpses into the work of the writer she would become, especially, and naturally I suppose, in her captions. Consider these delicious little O'Connor petards aimed at the walls of pretentiousness, academics, fashion, student politics, and student committees:

"It breaks my heart to leave for a whole summer."

"Do you have any books the faculty doesn't particularly recommend?"

"I don't enjoy looking at these old pictures either, but it doesn't hurt my reputation for people to think I'm a lover of fine arts."

"I think it's perfectly idiotic of the Navy not to let you WAVES dress sensibly like us college girls."

"I wonder if there could be anything to that business about studying at the first of the quarter?"

"Do you think teachers are necessary?"

"Understand, I got nothing against getting educated, but it just looks like there ought to be an easier way to do it."

"Targets Are Where You Find 'Em!"

"Wake me up in time to clap!"

But even though O'Connor's prints are unpolished, she maintains a technique that is consistent from one print to another, an accomplishment in itself. Most young printmakers can't decide whether to go this way or that, and end up going in many directions at the same time.

Obviously, she did not work from the live model or from any other form of visual reference to make these prints, and this is another part of their appeal. In 1963 she wrote Janet McKane, an epistolary friend in New York, about a self-portrait with a pheasant cock she had painted, saying that when she painted it, she did not look at herself in the mirror, nor did she look at the bird. "I knew what we both looked like," she wrote.[5]

Because her prints are not referential, I appreciate all the more her innate comprehension of *gesture*. I have taught life drawing for many years, and getting students to understand gesture is often the hardest part of the job. And it is that aspect of her graphic work that is most striking to me. Take a look at "Music Appreciation Hath Charms" and note how the right foot turns under the left foot of the character in the foreground. It is very natural, never mind the wanting of anatomical accuracy. Or note the wildly gyrating, dancing figures in

"These Two Express the Universal Feeling of Heart-Brokenness Over School Closing." In the other prints: the naturalness of figures walking, reading a newspaper, carrying a heavy burden, scratching the head, nursing a sore back, leaning against a post, strutting, standing at attention or at a lectern. I could go on, but it is this sense of gesture that shows me that she knew, or at least understood — perhaps below her level of awareness — what she was doing, regardless of the degree of sophistication of the image itself.

Much can be forgiven in drawing the human figure if the gesture is right. Conversely, if the figure is rendered competently and the gesture is wrong, then the whole thing is wrong. This understanding of gesture flows over into her fiction. Take for example the problem she has about the final meeting of Mrs. May and the bull in her short story "Greenleaf": "My preoccupations," she wrote to her friend Betty Hester, "are technical. My preoccupation is how am I going to get this bull's horns into this woman's ribs?"[6]

Indeed. It's all a matter of gesture.[7] O'Connor also had a strong, natural sense of composition that becomes evident after studying the prints. The overall pattern of "Oh, well, I can always be a Ph.D.," is a good example. She divides the rectangle into many near-repetitive black shapes, contrasts them with smaller, similar shapes in white, and then throws in a series of circle-like shapes and bold, angular stripes — all in all it reminds me, distantly, of Pablo Picasso's *Girl Before a Mirror* (1932), or Marsden Hartley's *Portrait of a German Officer* (1914), or George Grosz's *The Guilty One Remains Unknown* (1919).

In a letter to Robie Macauley dated October 13, 1953, O'Connor says that she read Joseph Conrad's novels because she hoped "they'll affect my writing without my being bothered knowing how."[8] I wonder how much time she spent looking at the work of other artists and, if she did, just how much of it rubbed off on her without her being bothered knowing how. Likely as not, she taught that chicken to walk backward without being bothered to know how either. It was her way.

BELOW: The entrance to the college was marked by a sign suspended from cables, as shown in this photo from the cover of a 1946 *Alumnae Journal*. O'Connor incorporates this campus landmark into a 1944 cartoon commenting on the school's conservative rules, an incendiary issue in the student government association elections that spring.

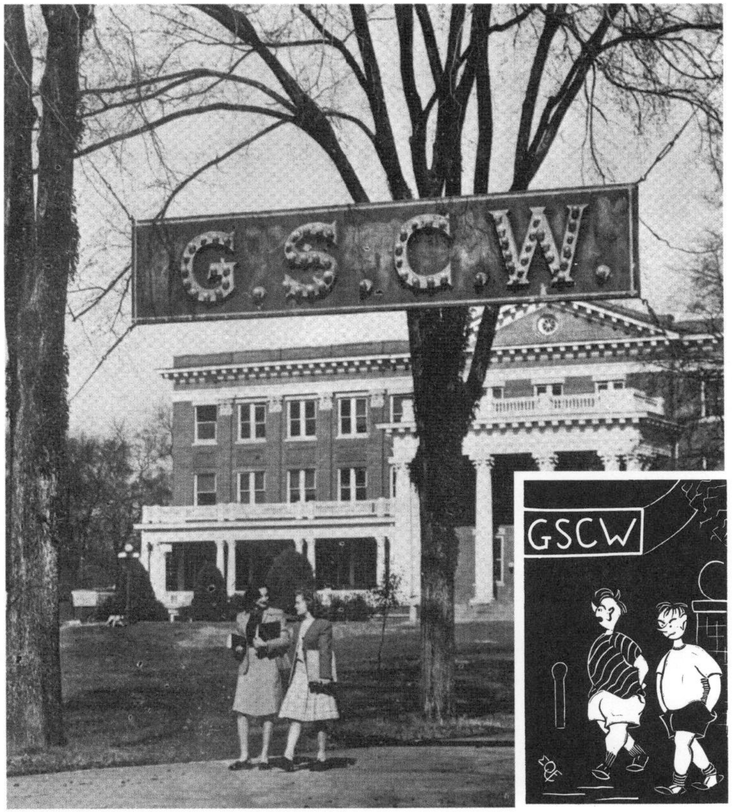
G.S.C.W.
GSCW

1 Flannery O'Connor, quoted in *Conversations with Flannery O'Connor*, ed. Rosemary M. Magee (Jackson: University Press of Mississippi, 1987), 38.

2 I saw an exhibit of prints from behind the Iron Curtain at the University of Nebraska. A few were linoleum cuts done with a hypodermic needle and were extraordinarily fine. Leonard Baskin made a few linoleum engravings, but these are highly unusual.

3 O'Connor to Betty Hester, November 25, 1955, *The Habit of Being: Letters of Flannery O'Connor*, ed. Sally Fitzgerald (New York: Farrar, Straus and Giroux, 1979), 116.

4 O'Connor to Betty Hester, December 1959, *Habit of Being*, 362.

5 O'Connor to Janet McKane, June 19, 1963, *Habit of Being*, 525.

6 O'Connor to Betty Hester, March 24, 1956, *Habit of Being*, 149.

7 While I do enjoy the humor and directness of her prints, she is working on a much higher artistic plane when she draws. Those three splendid continuous line drawings of a flower and the nun's headgear [p. 112, 129] make me want to see more.

8 O'Connor to Robie Macauley, October 13, 1953, *Habit of Being*, 63.

THE CARTOONS

THE CARTOONS

From *The Peabody Palladium*   2 | 3

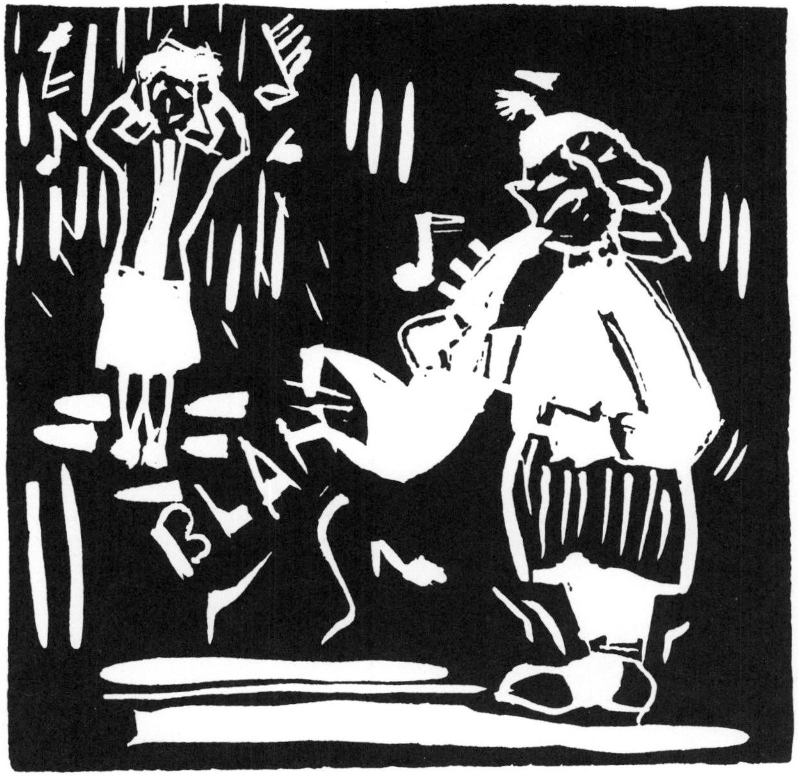
BLA

One Result of the New Peabody Orchestra

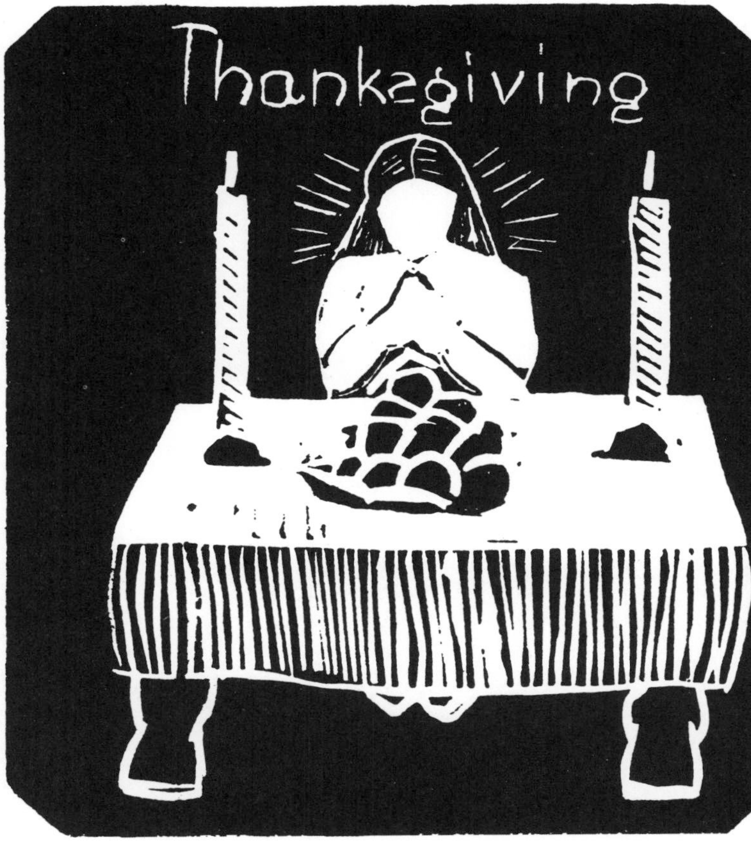
Thanksgiving

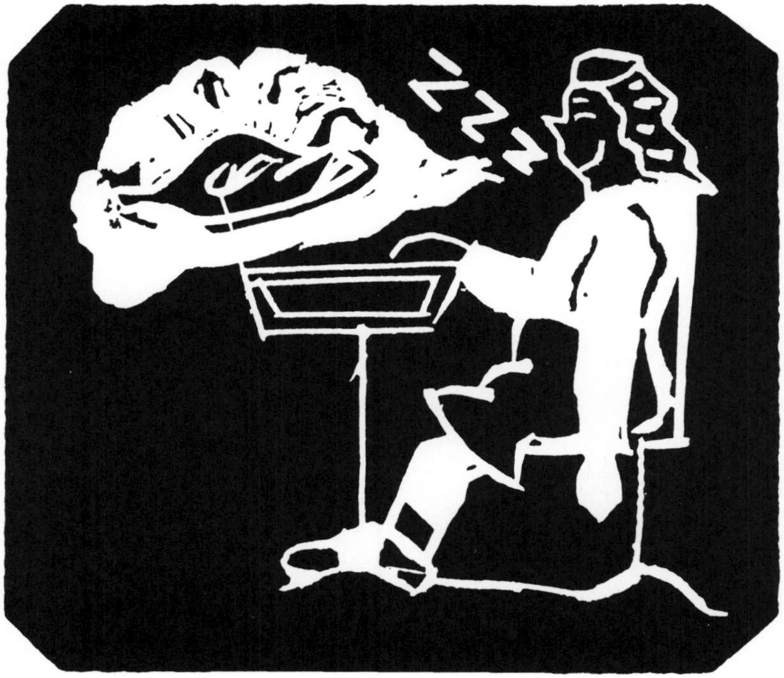
ZZZ

Just One More Day To Dream

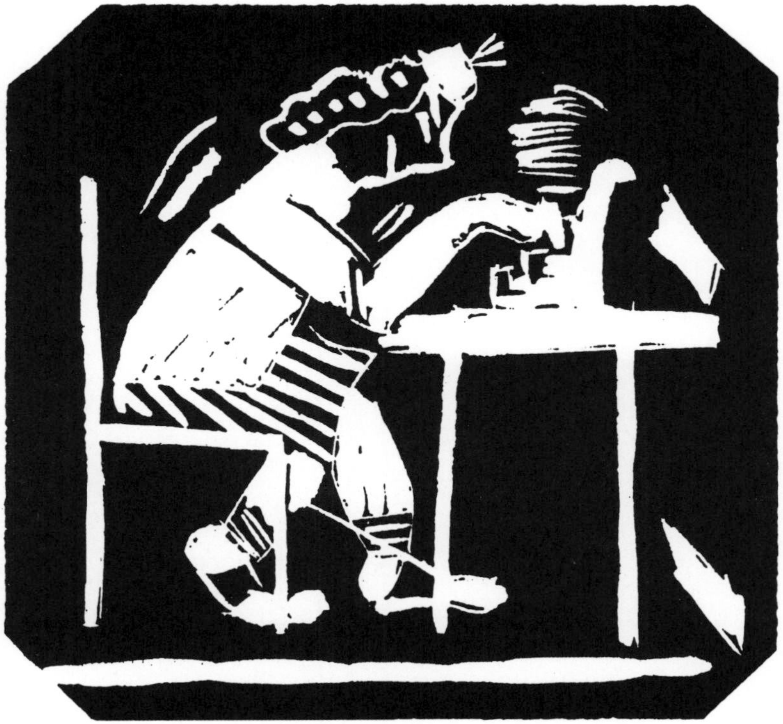

'Twas the Night Before Press Time

The Wrong Way To Do It

Senior, Senior, Wherefore Art Thou, Senior?

Now Comes Spring Fever

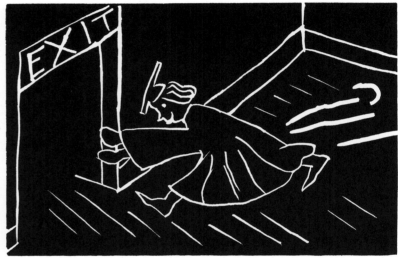

At Long Last...

In Hopes That a Jimmie Soon Will Be There

Music Appreciation Hath Charms

These Two Express the Universal Feeling of
Heart-Brokenness Over School Closing

From *The Colonnade*   14 | 15

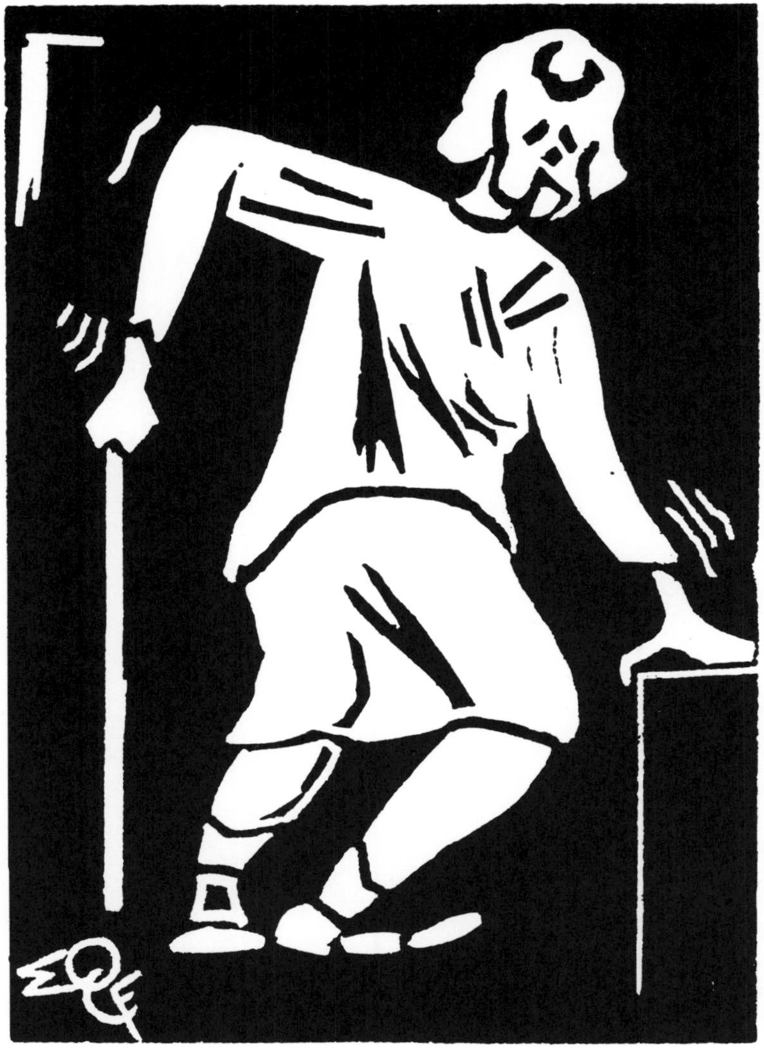

The Immediate Results of Physical Fitness Day

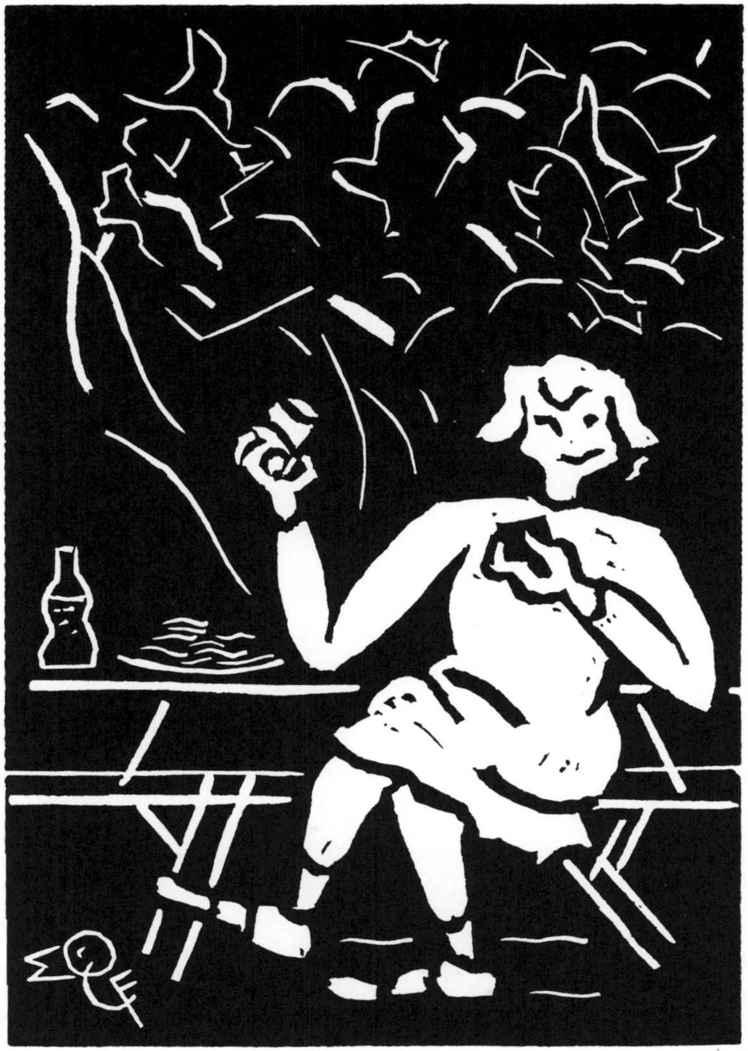

Why Don't We Do This More Often?

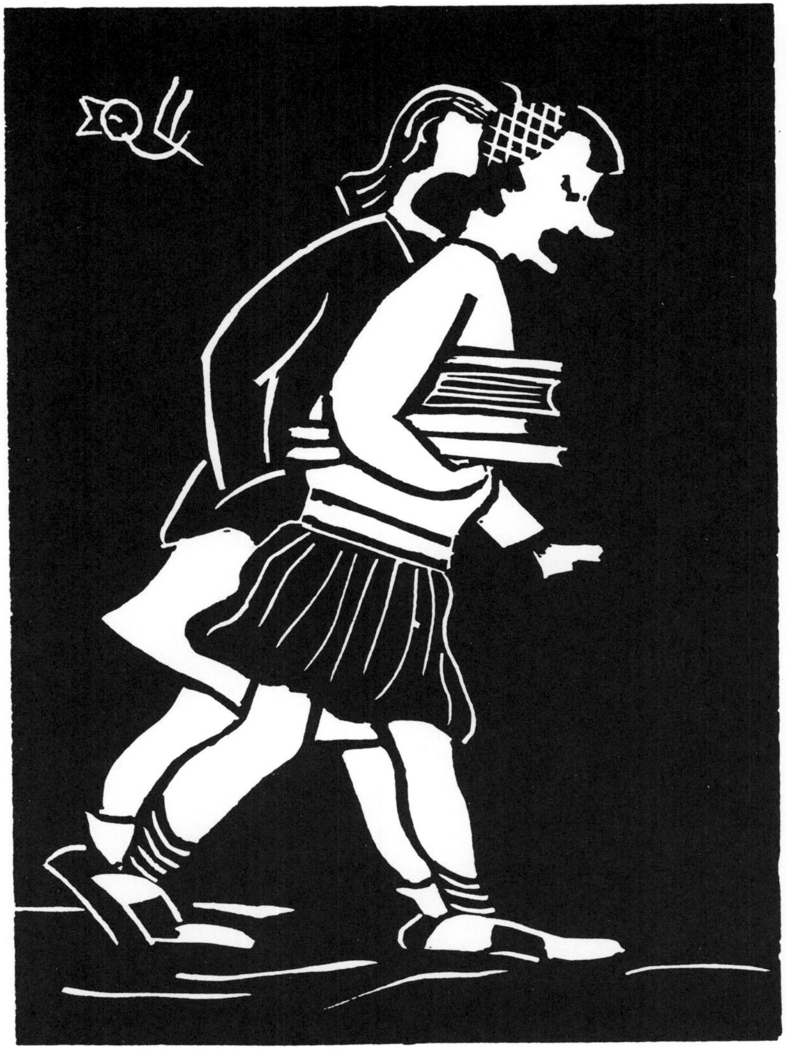

"Aw nuts, I thought we'd have at least one day off after the faculty played softball."

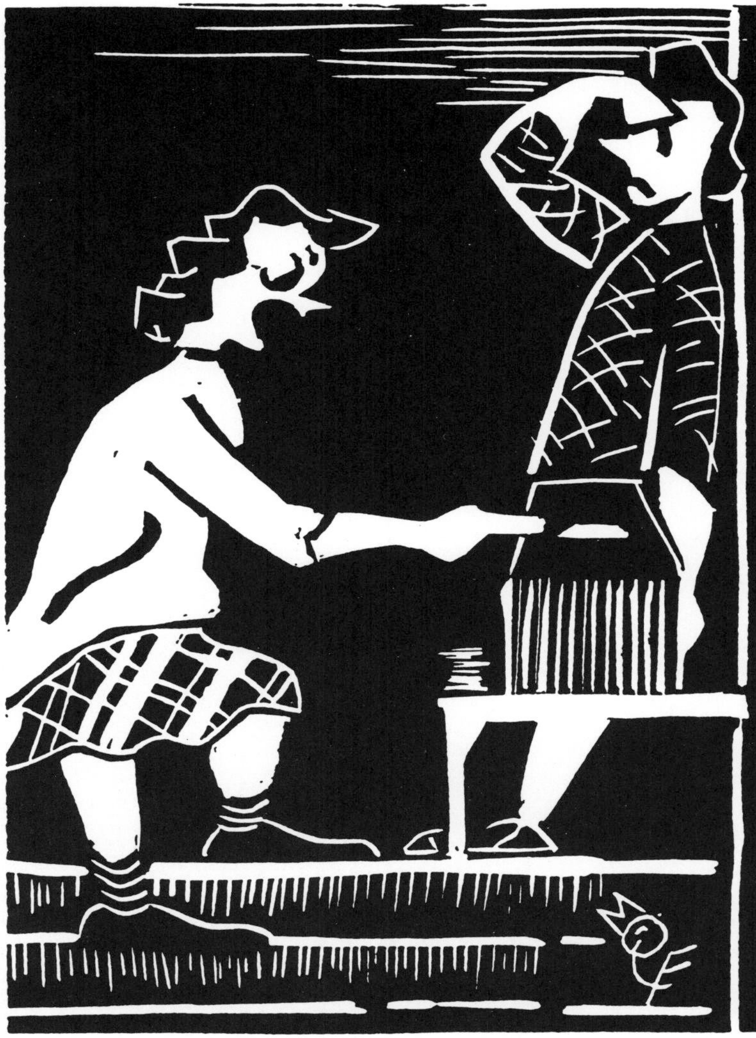

"Oh, gosh! I didn't know you had to pay a poll tax."

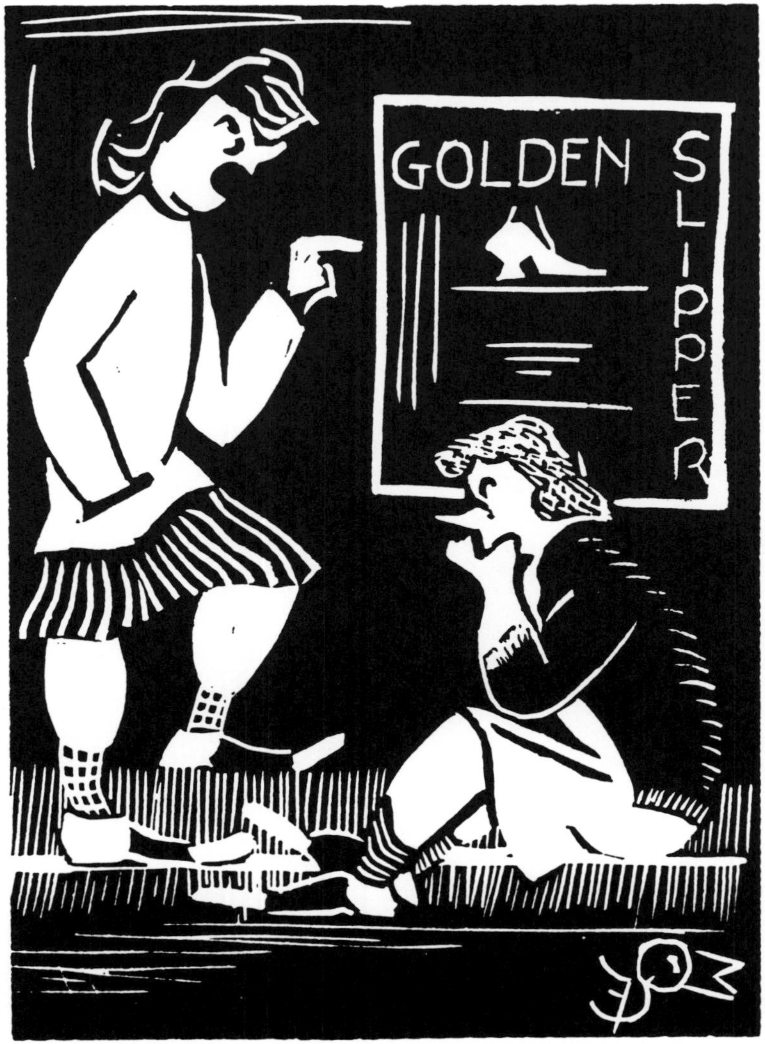
GOLDEN SLIPPER

"Doggone this Golden Slipper Contest. Now we have to wear saddle oxfords."

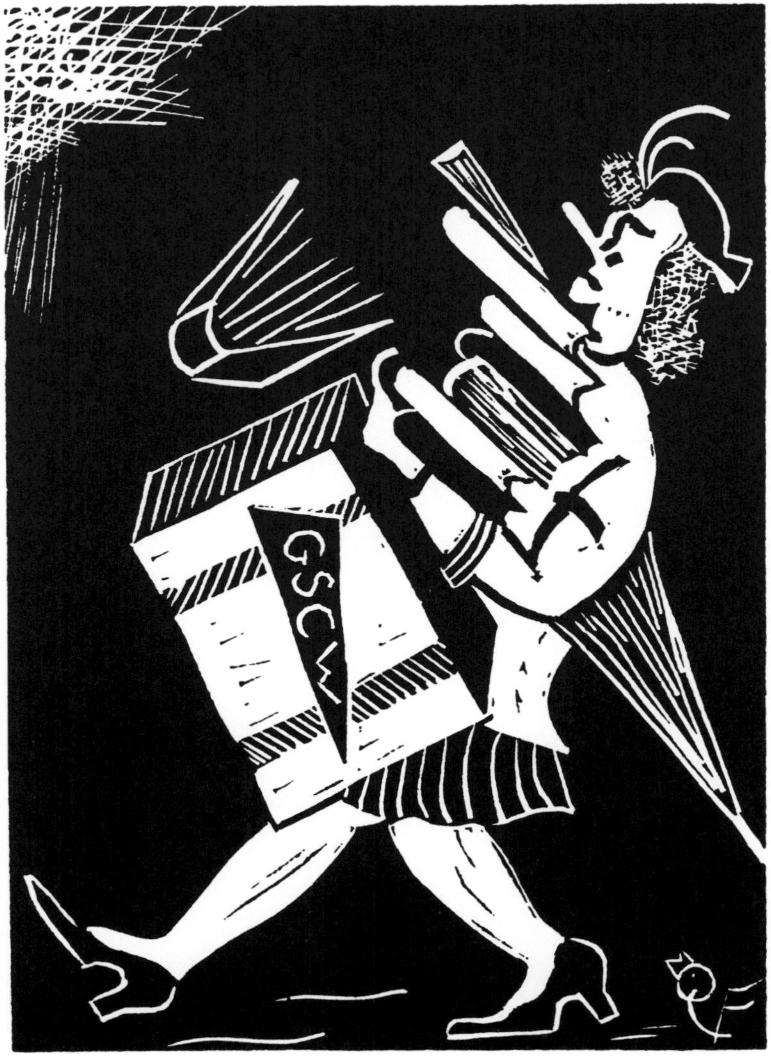
GSCW

Term Papers Add Quite a Lot to These Thanksgiving Holidays

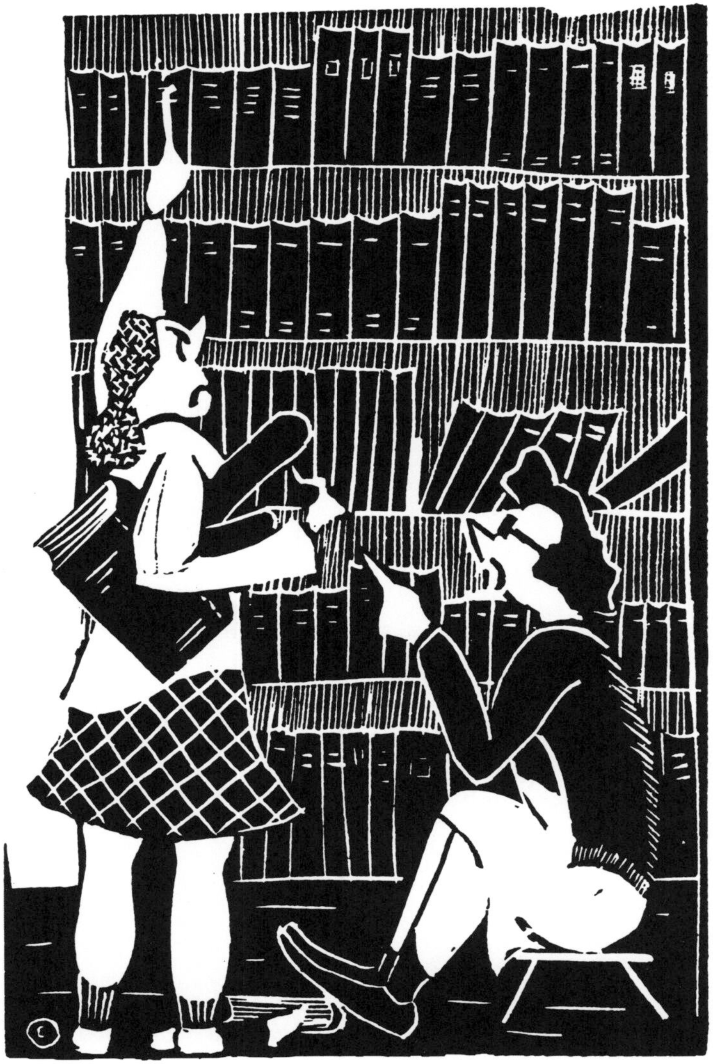

“Are you glad to be back?”

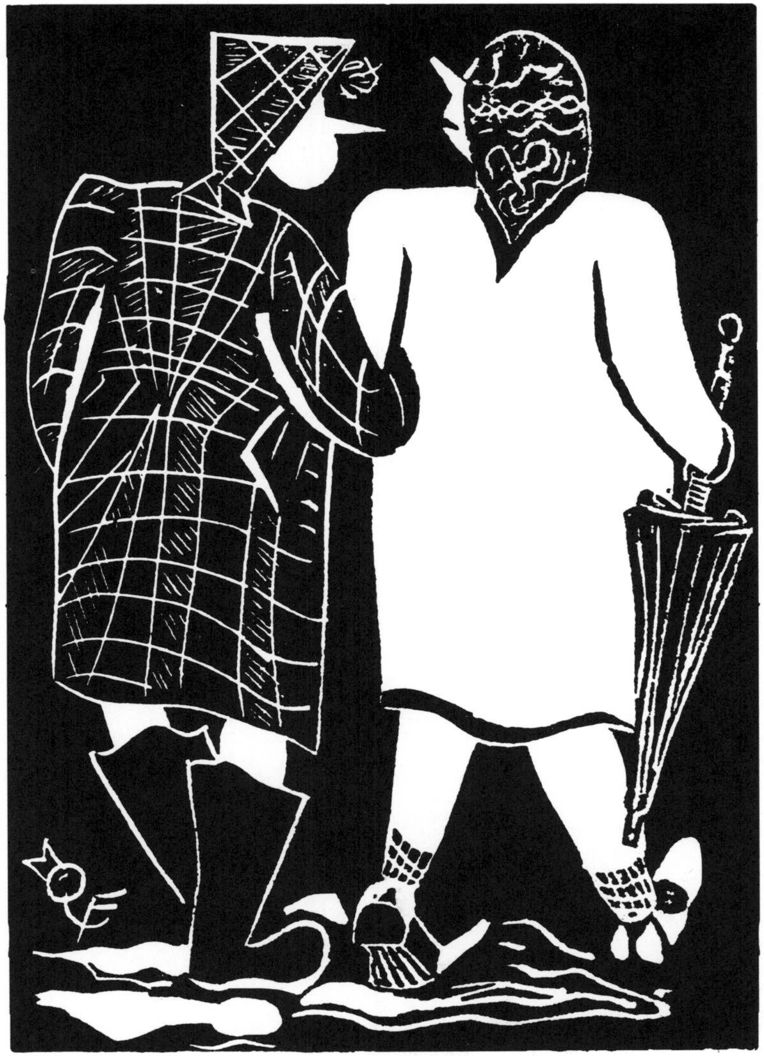

“In the light of our common knowledge, don’t you consider this examination business rather superfluous?”

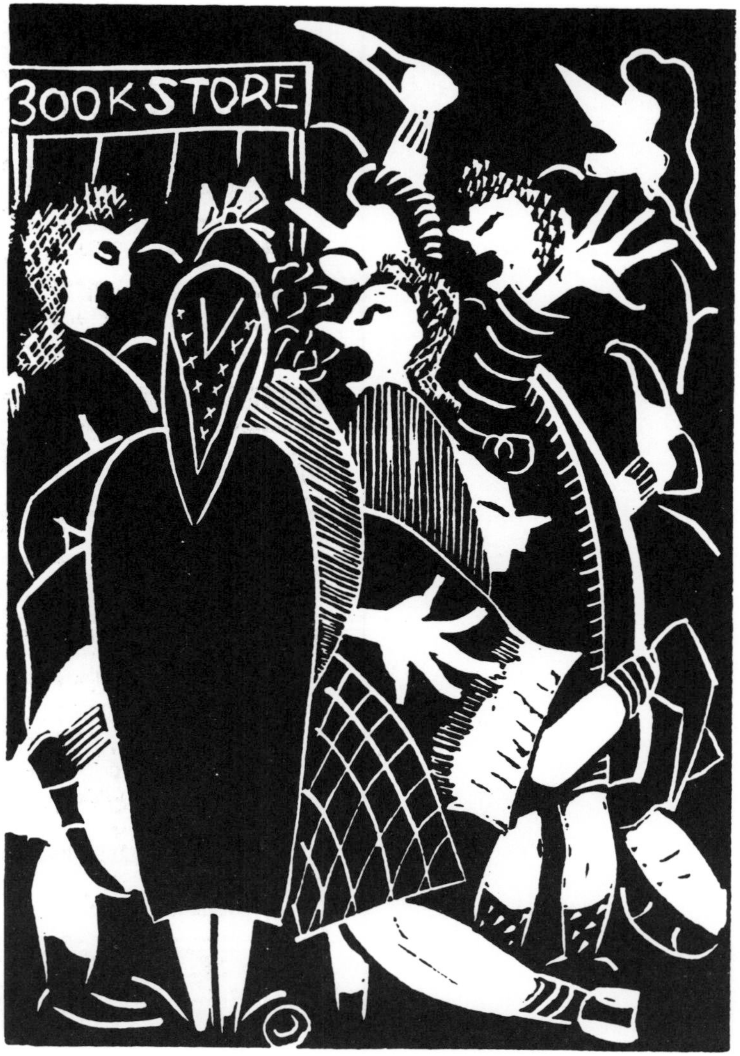
BOOK STORE

Business as Usual

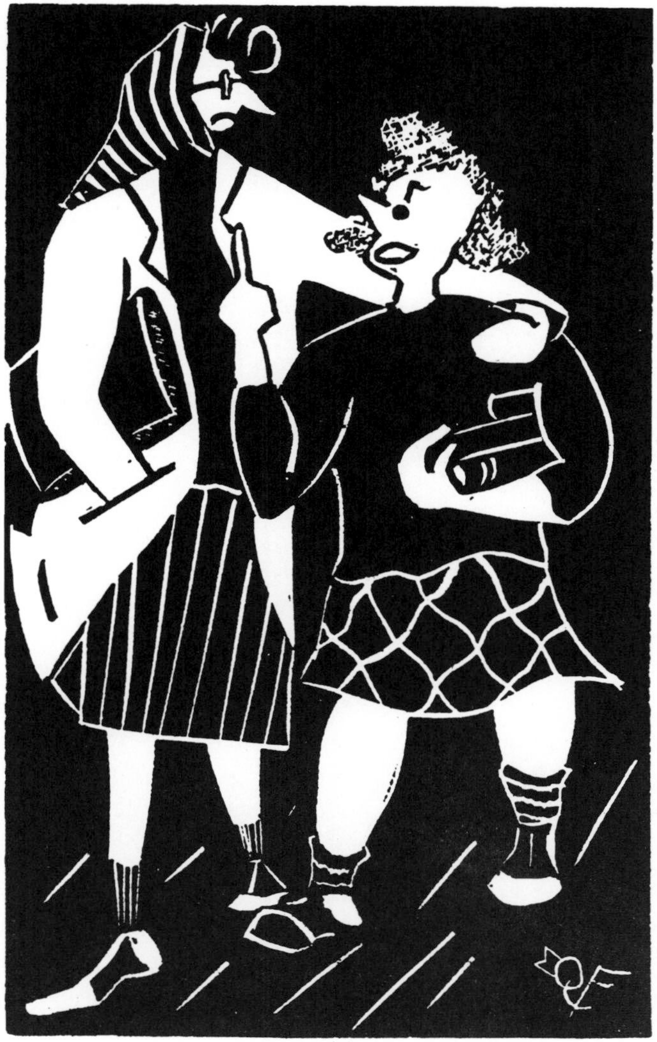

"Aw, don't worry about not getting on the Dean's List. It's no fun going to the picture show at night anyway."

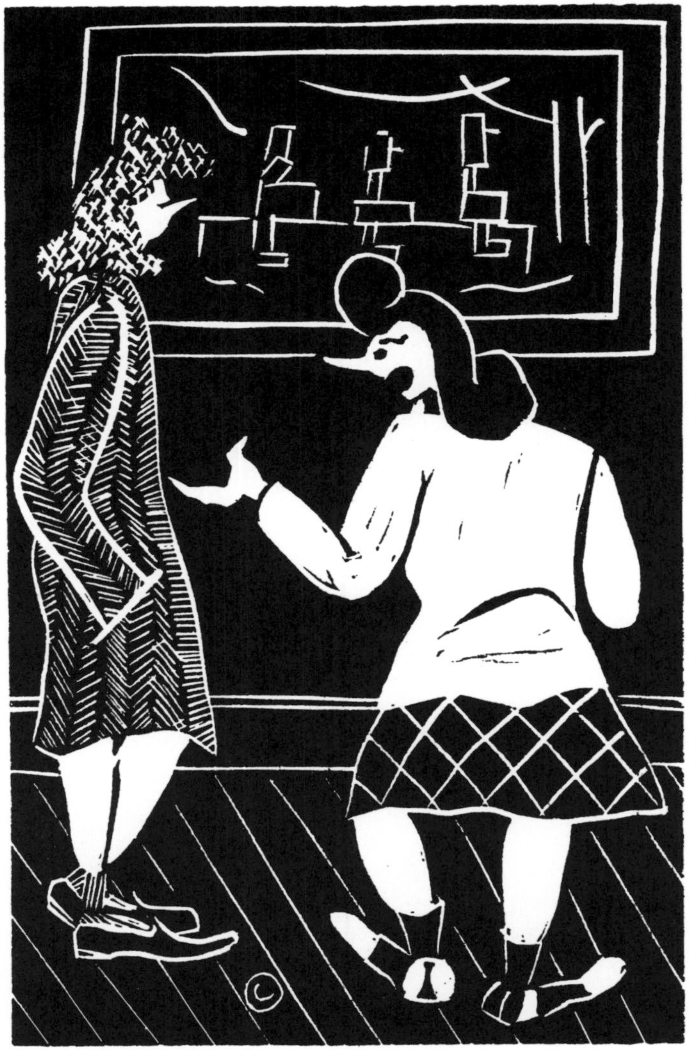

"I don't enjoy looking at these old pictures either,
but it doesn't hurt my reputation for people to think
I'm a lover of fine arts."

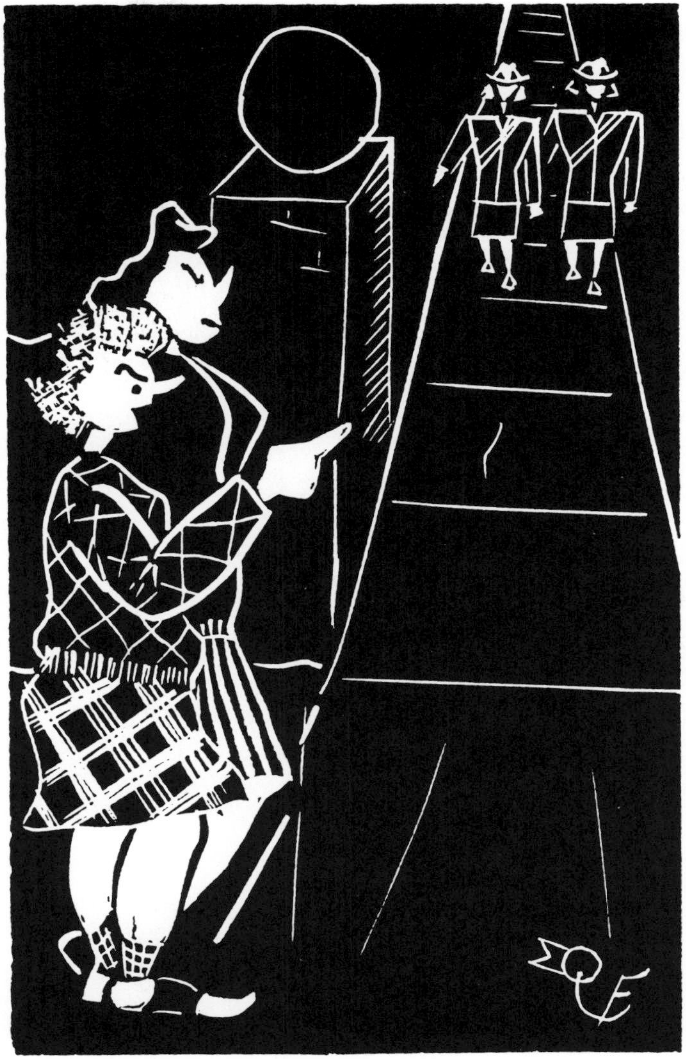

"Officer or no officer, I'm going to ask her
to let me try on that hat."

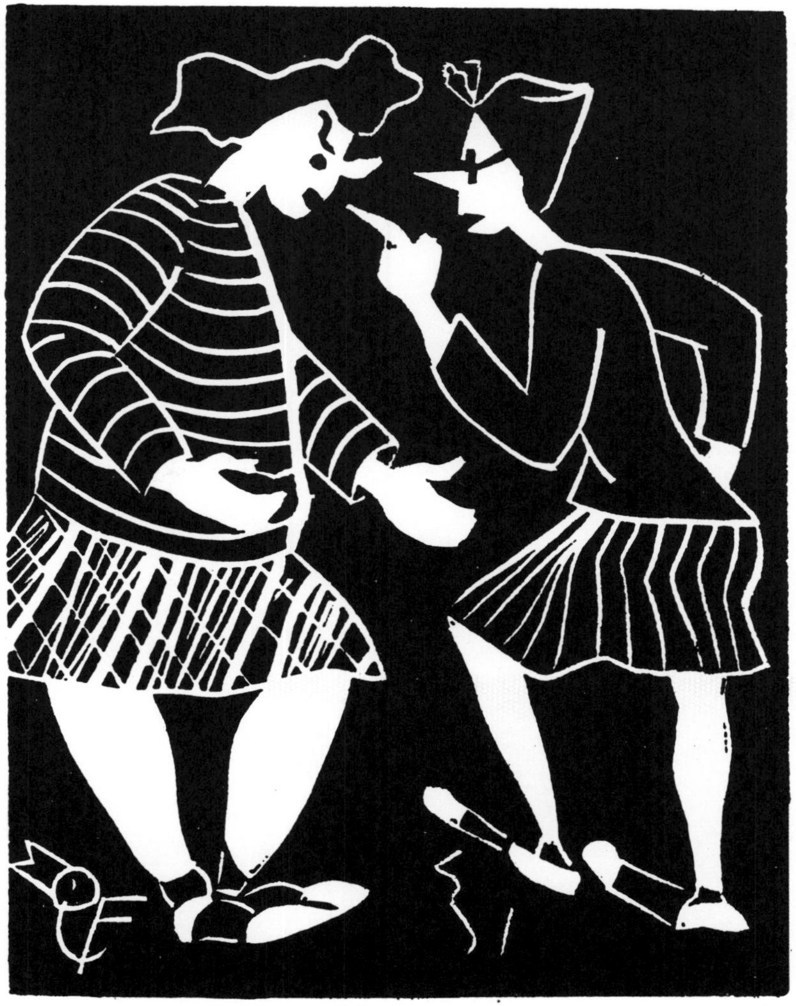

"But I tell you, you don't have to get a rooster to tell when to get up; all you have to do is set your clock back."

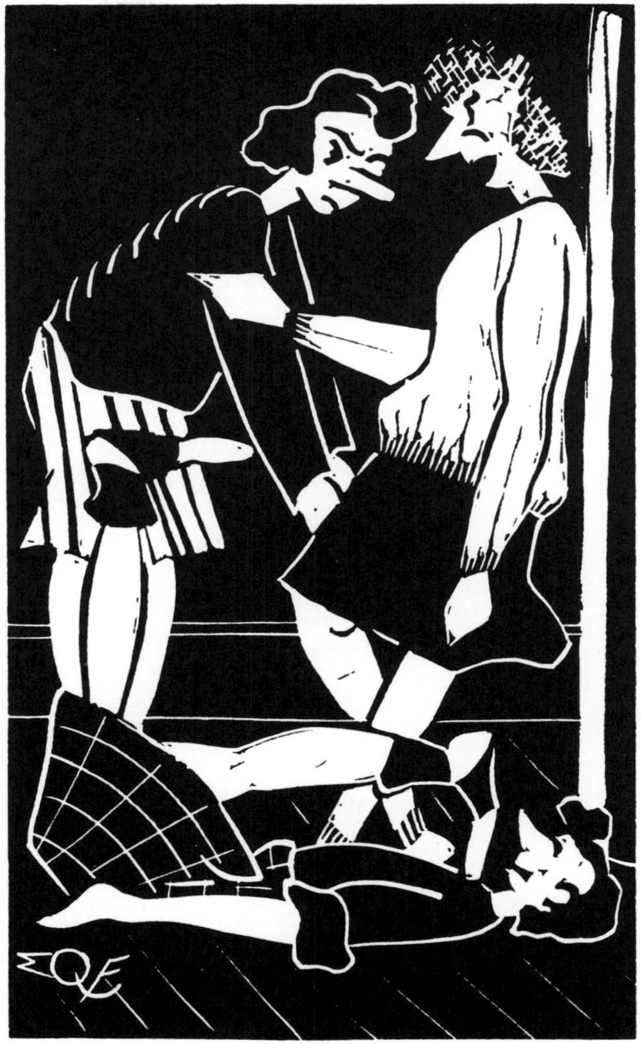

"Now why waste all your energy getting physically fit? You'll never look like a WAVE anyhow."

Traffic

"See there, I told you they didn't keep gunpowder
in those things."

"It's a shame nobody petitioned me for an office. I could have done much more for Faculty-Student relations."

"Oh, give me back my raincoat; you still look more like a moron than a WAVE."

"Coming back affects some people worse than others."

Targets Are Where You Find 'Em!

"Oh, well, I can always be a Ph.D."

"I think it's perfectly idiotic of the Navy not to let you
WAVES dress sensibly like us college girls."

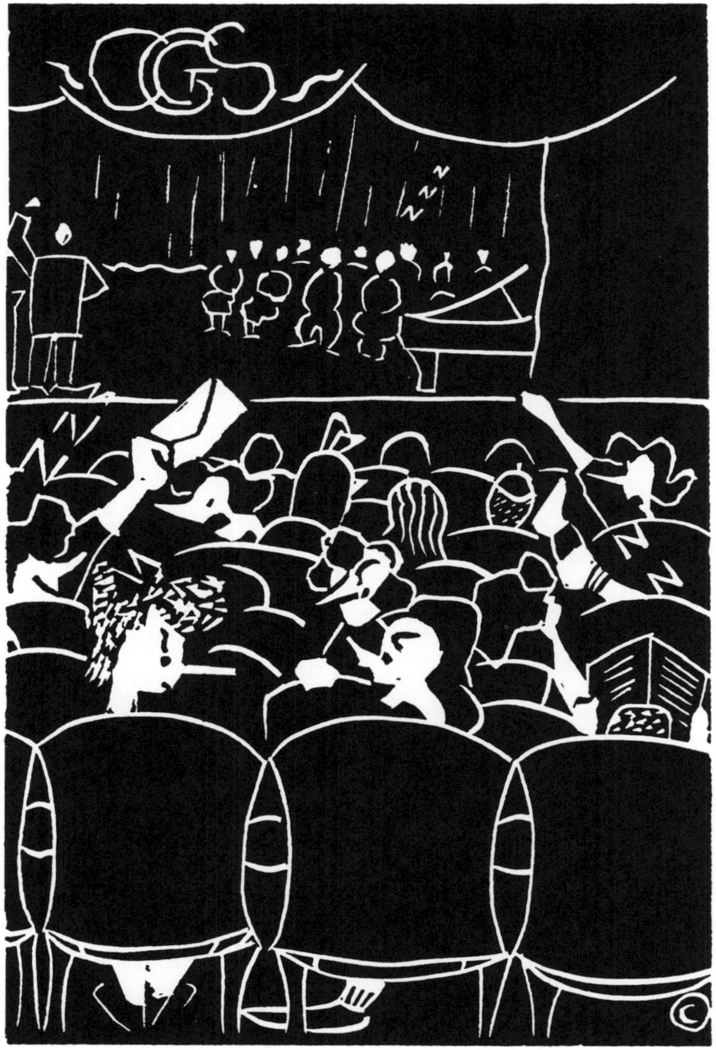
CGS

"Wake me up in time to clap!"

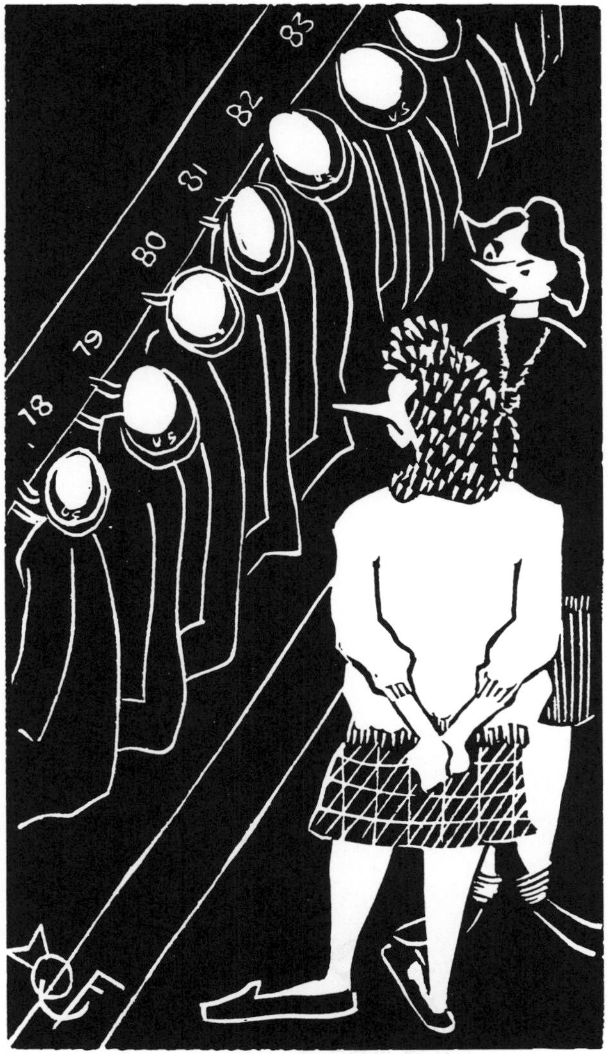
18
79
80
81
82
83

"If we moved all those hats on the wrong hooks, do you think we'd still be eligible for the Dean's List?"

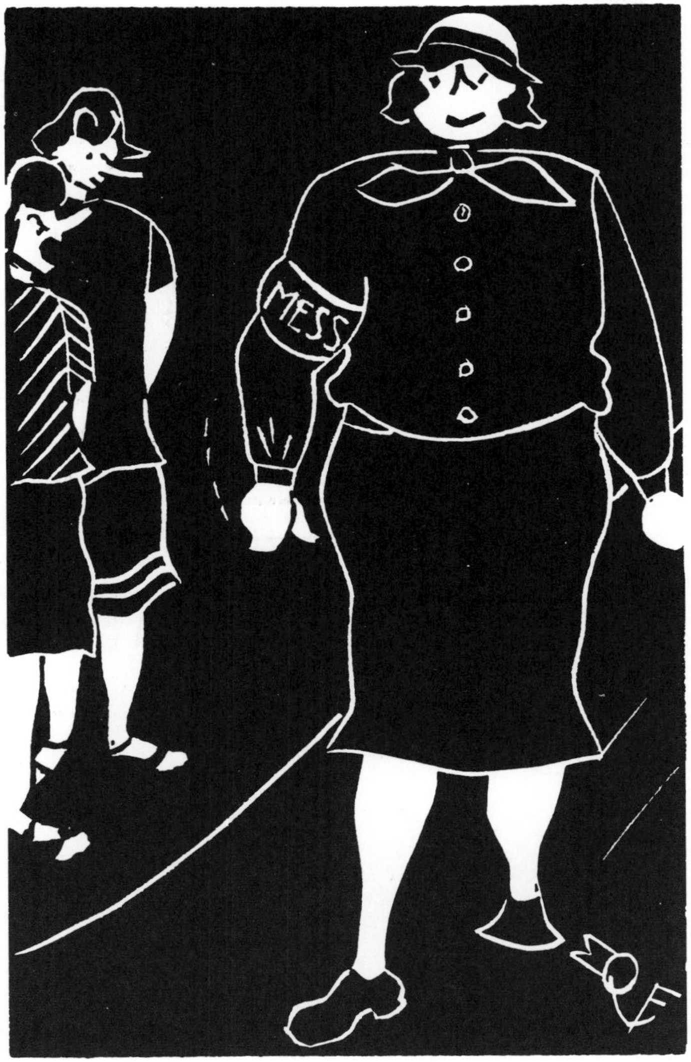
MESS

"Aw, quit trying to tell me that thing means she's a *messenger*. I'm not so dumb."

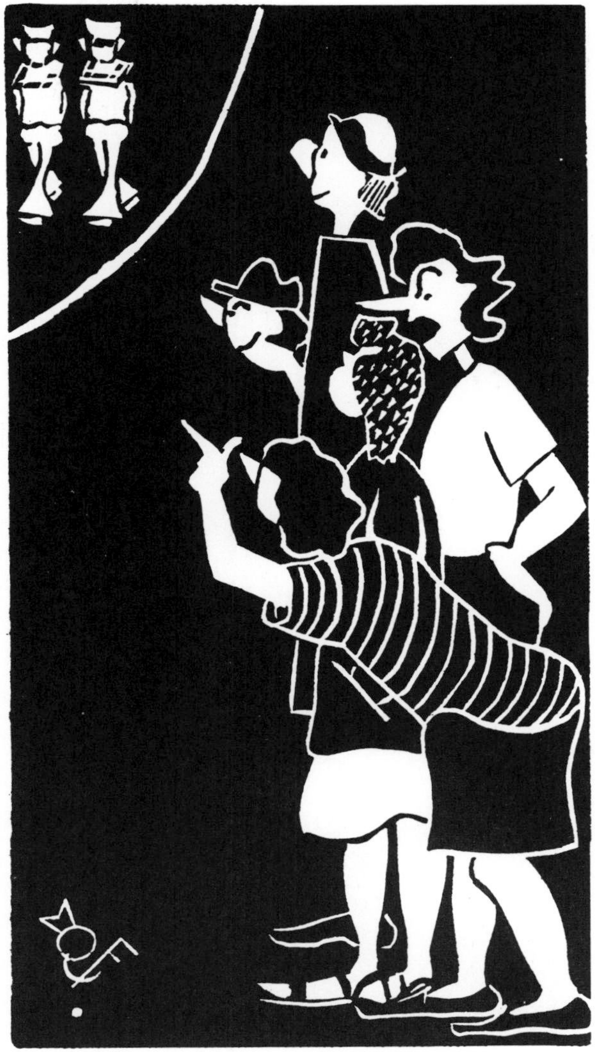

"Those are the kind of WAVES I like."

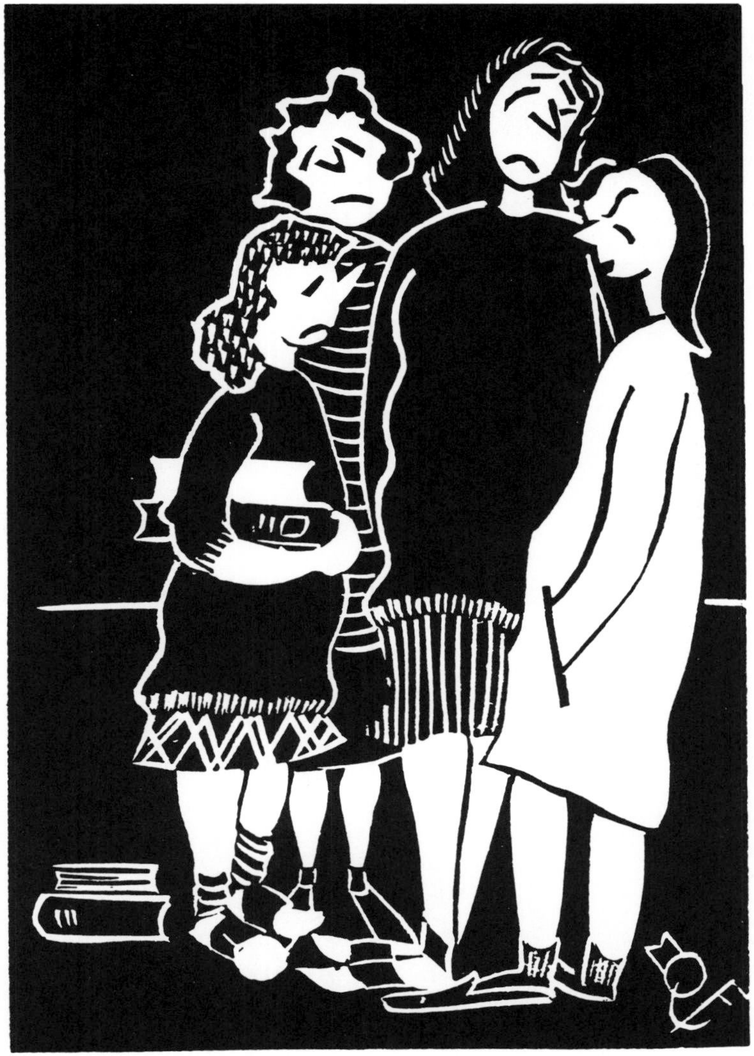

"Gosh, we're glad to be back."

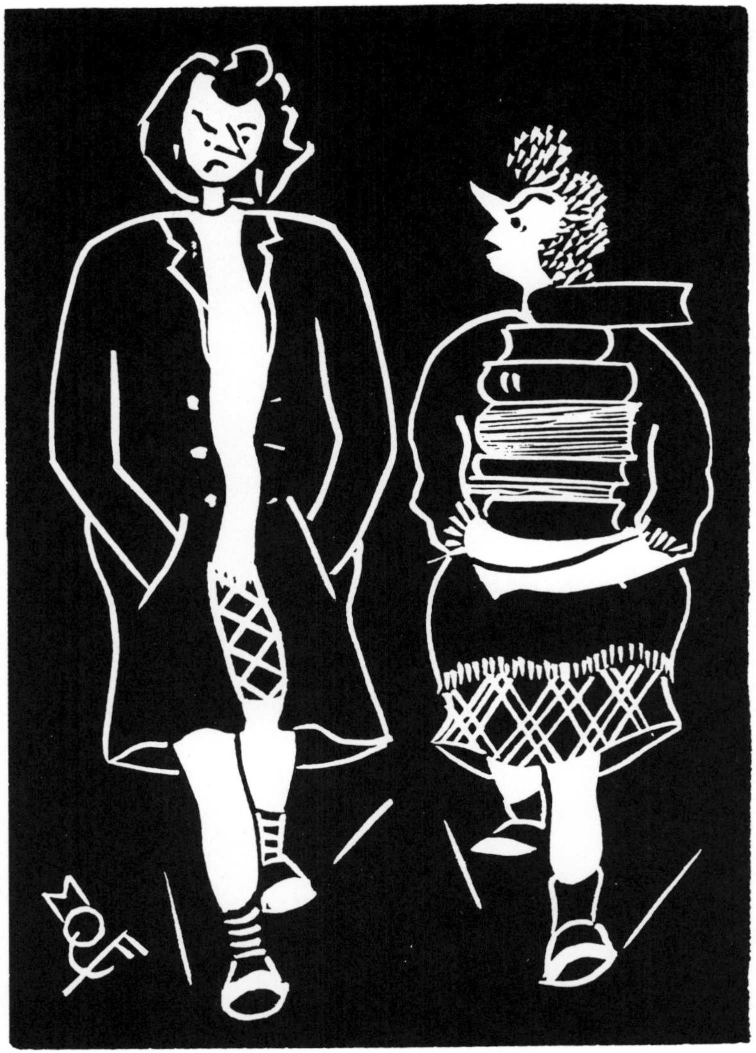

"Do you think teachers are necessary?"

"They are giving us entirely too much work. Why, I don't
have time for but six outside activities!"

"Could I interest you in buying a
Contemporary Georgia syllabus?"

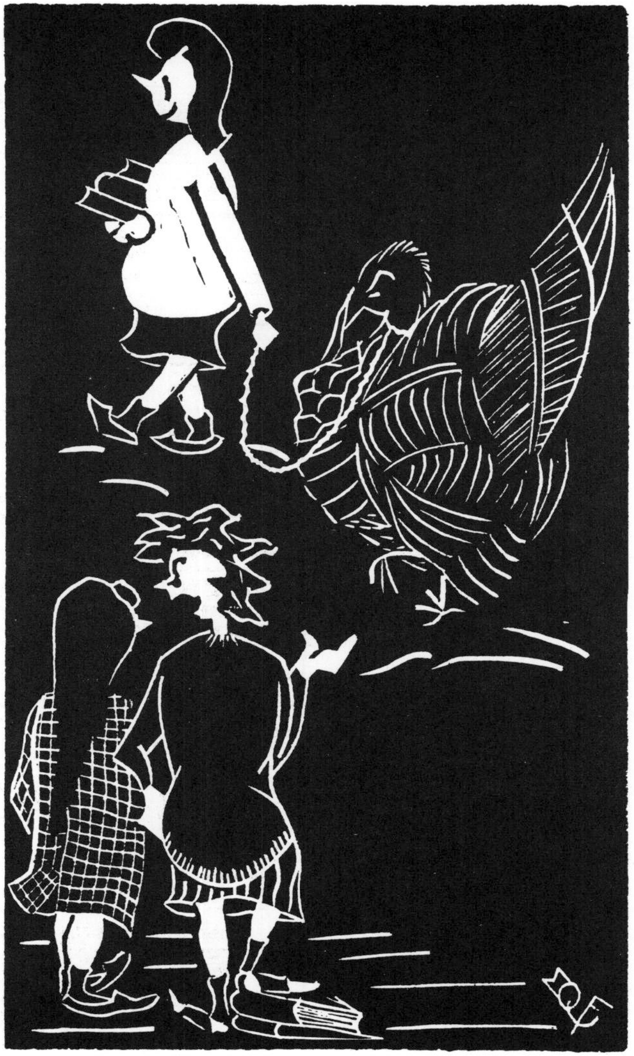

"Just the thought of getting away from here for a few days unhinges some people, you know."

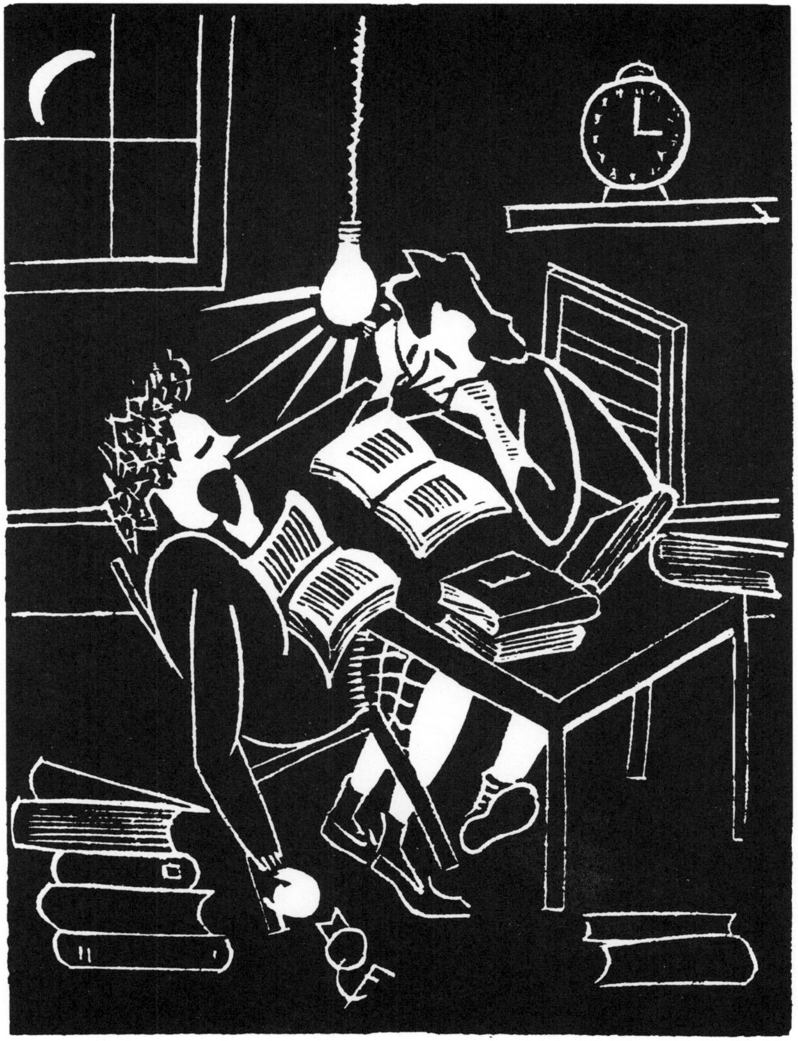

"I wonder if there could be anything to that business about studying at the first of the quarter?"

"I hear there's a shortage of classrooms."

This Can Never Be Done in Ten Minutes

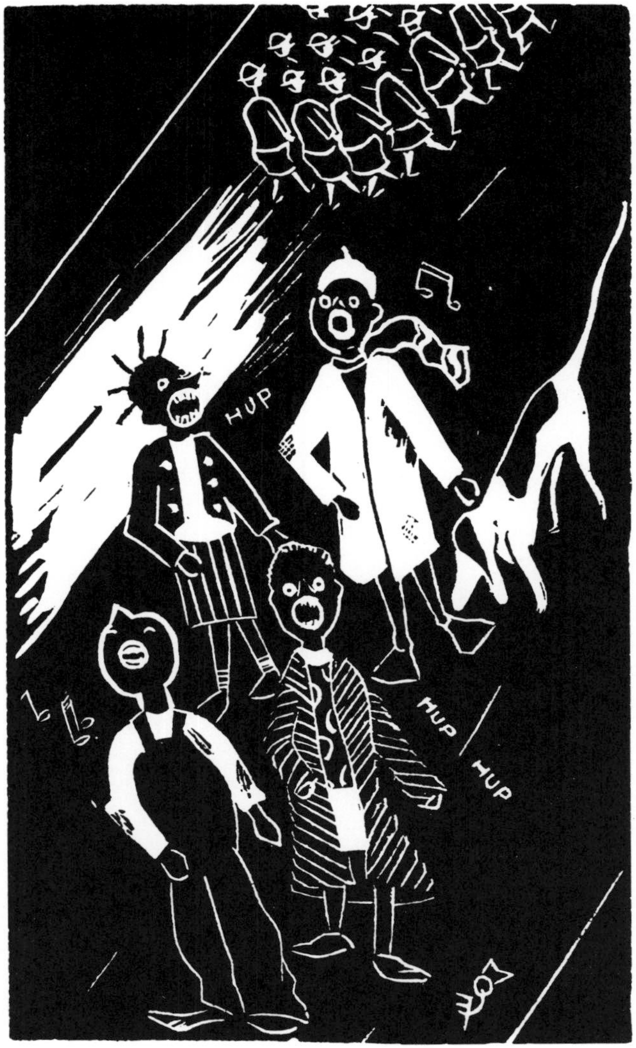
HUP
HUP
HUP

"Two mo' monts we won' be a-doin' it . . . ."

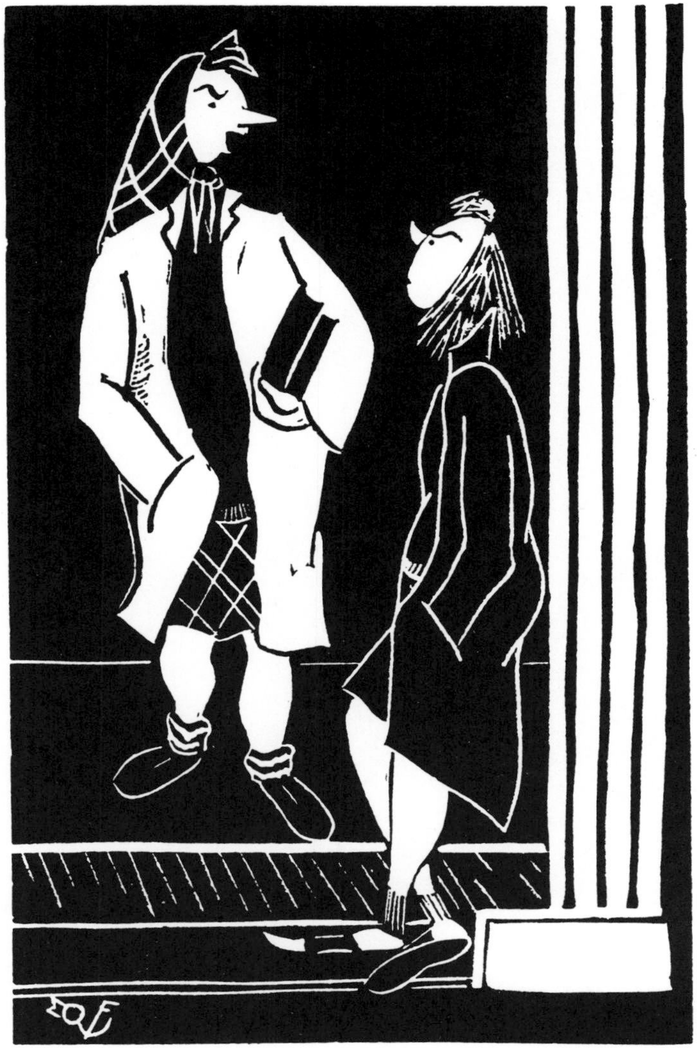

"Kilpatrick was fair."

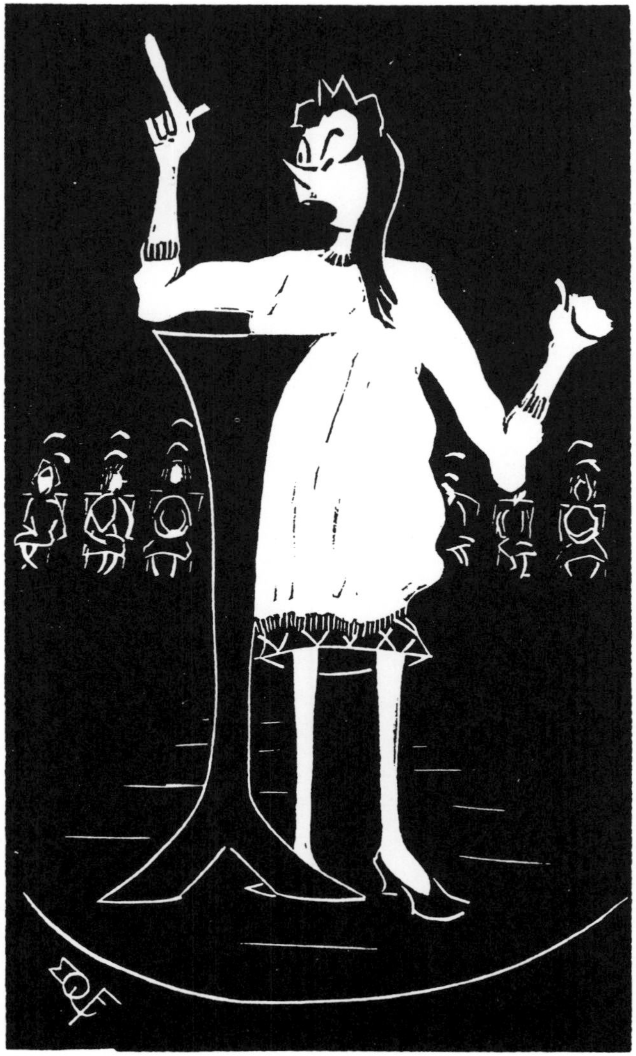

"I believe the totalitarian outlook of the aggresive minority
in the educational-governmental faction should be crushed,
and if I am elected sixth vice recording secretary,
I shall bend every effort to crush it."

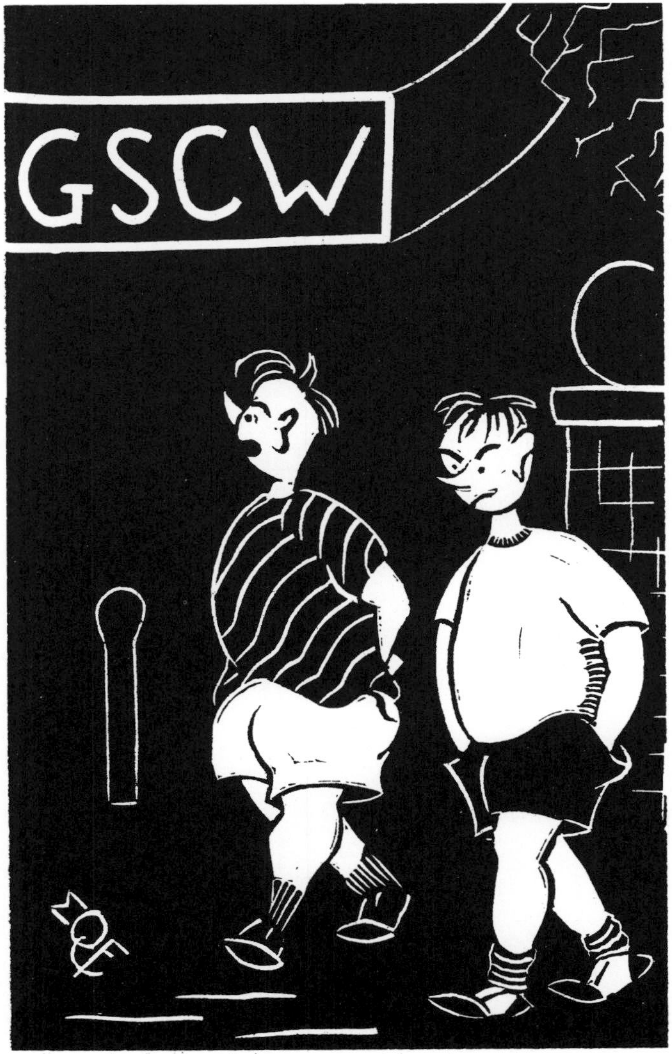
GSCW

"I hope the rules of that place slacken up before
we start going out with girls."

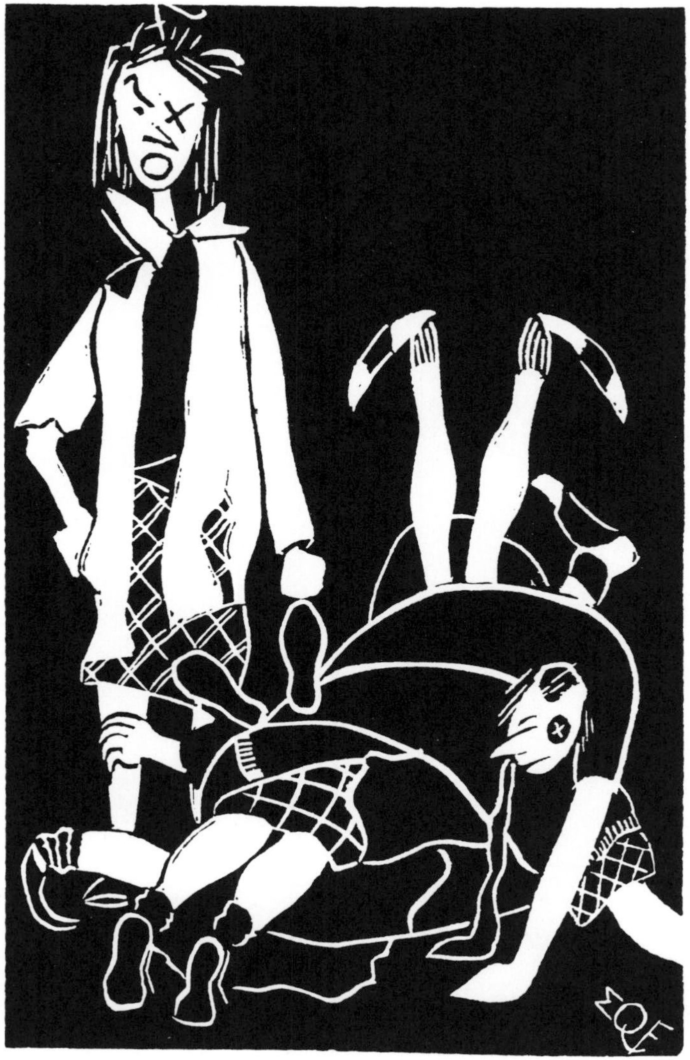

"Madam Chairman, the committee has reached a decision."

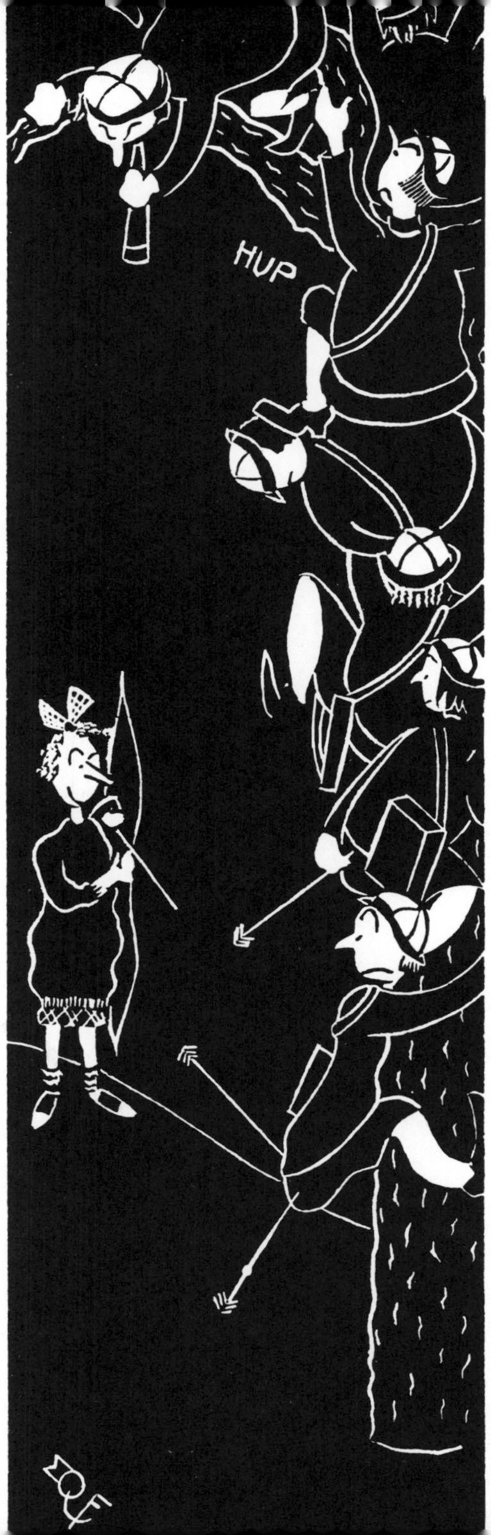
HUP

Counter-Attack

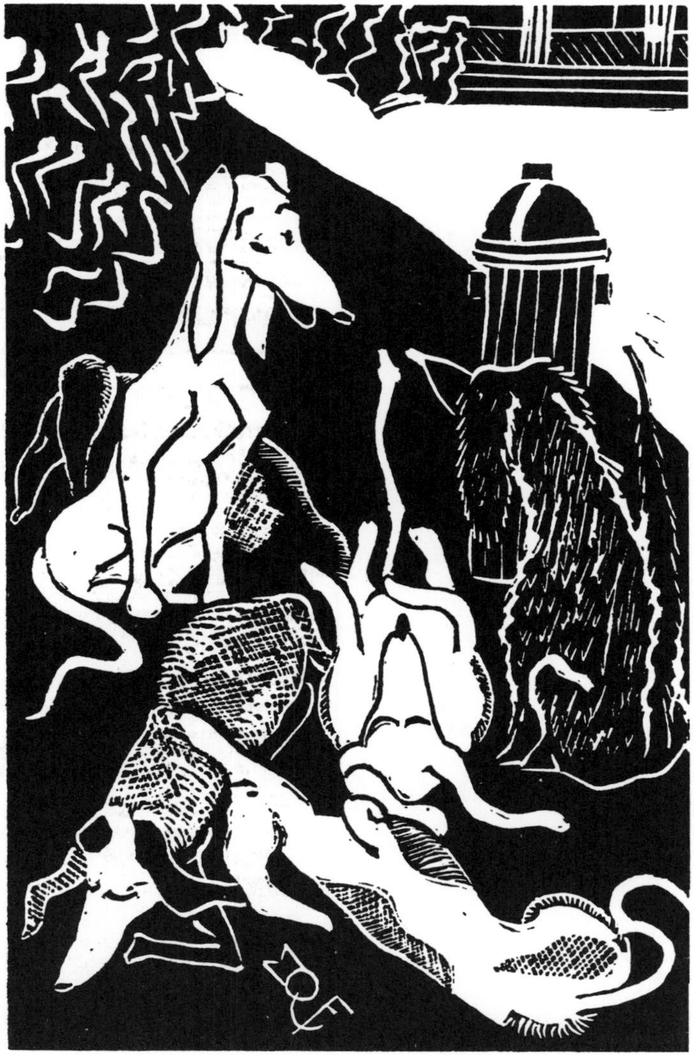

"The whole family's been wintering here at GSCW—
you have to take what you can get these days."

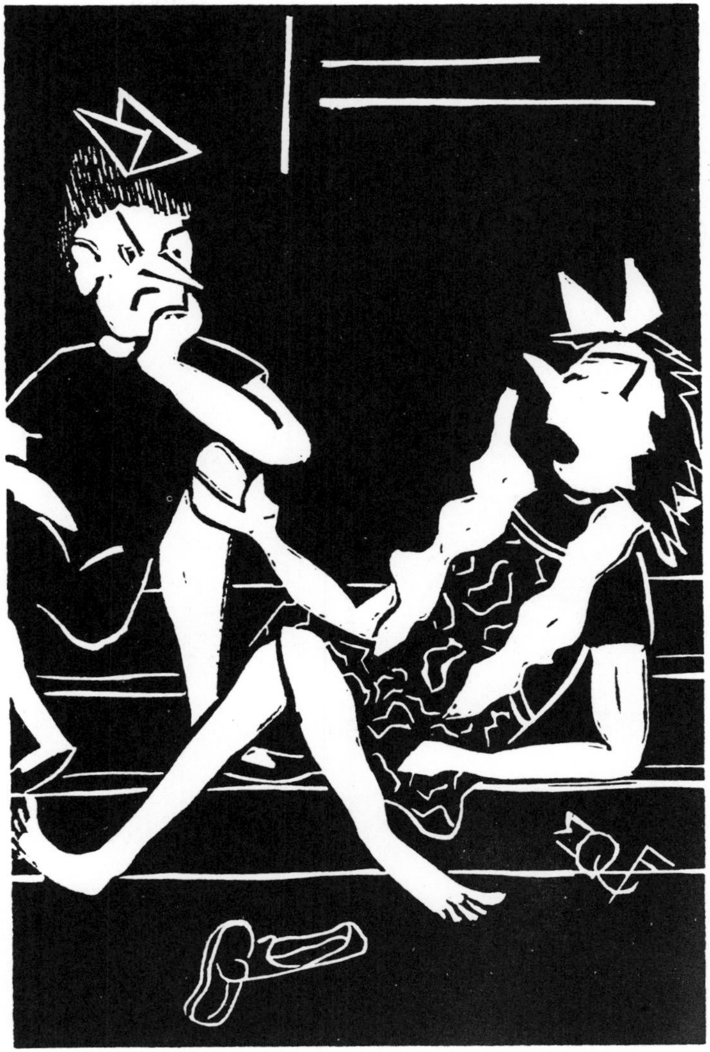

"This place will never amount to anything until they get
a Student Committee on Faculty Relations."

"It breaks my heart to leave for a whole summer."

"I understand it's a form of physic maladjustment created by a marked dissatisfaction with a change in environment wherein the family unit is disrupted—called homesickness."

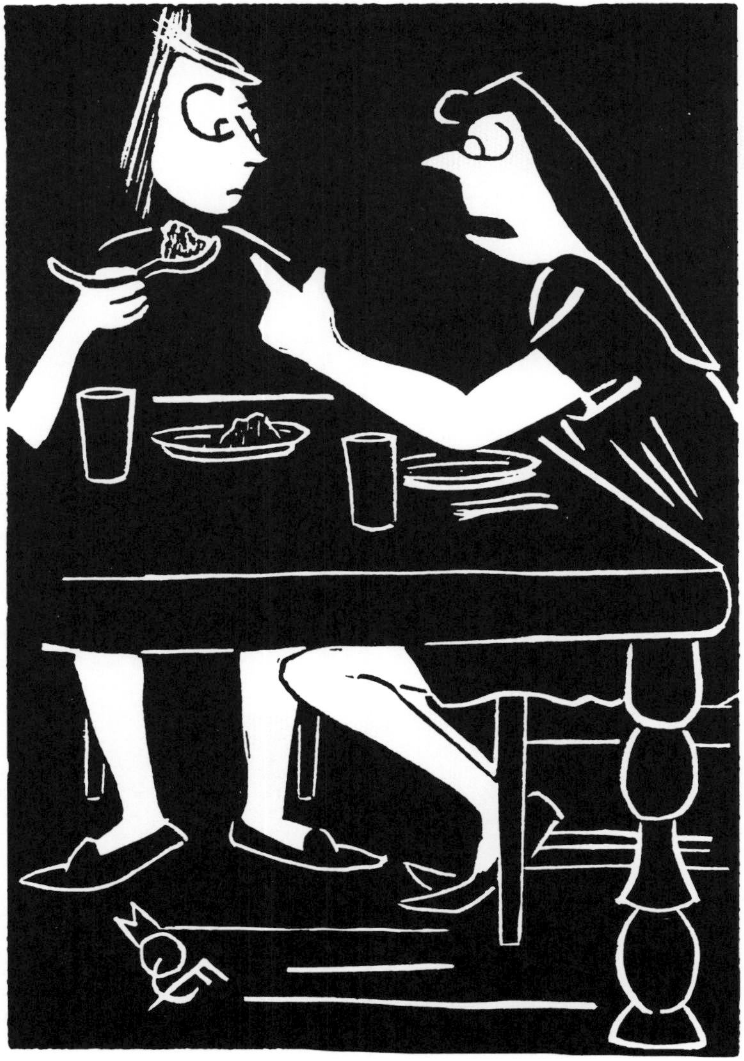

"Now if 50,000 paratyphoid bacillae can go through the eye of a needle abreast, that ought to put at least 500,000,000,000 in that spoonful; and you should be ill by early tomorrow morning."

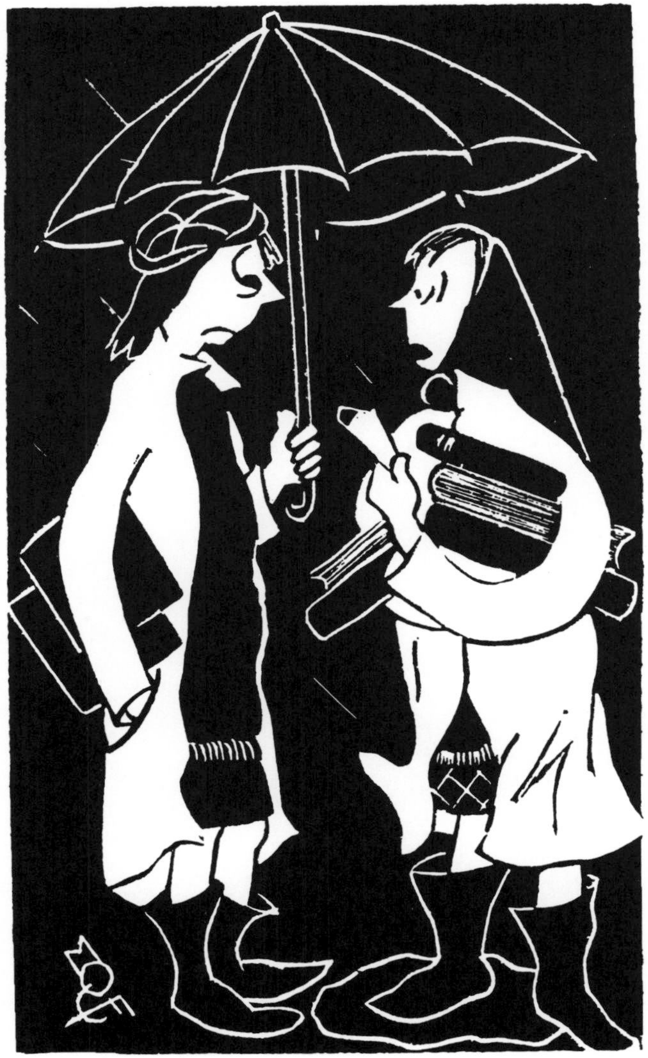

"Understand, I got nothing against getting educated, but it just looks like there ought to be an easier way to do it."

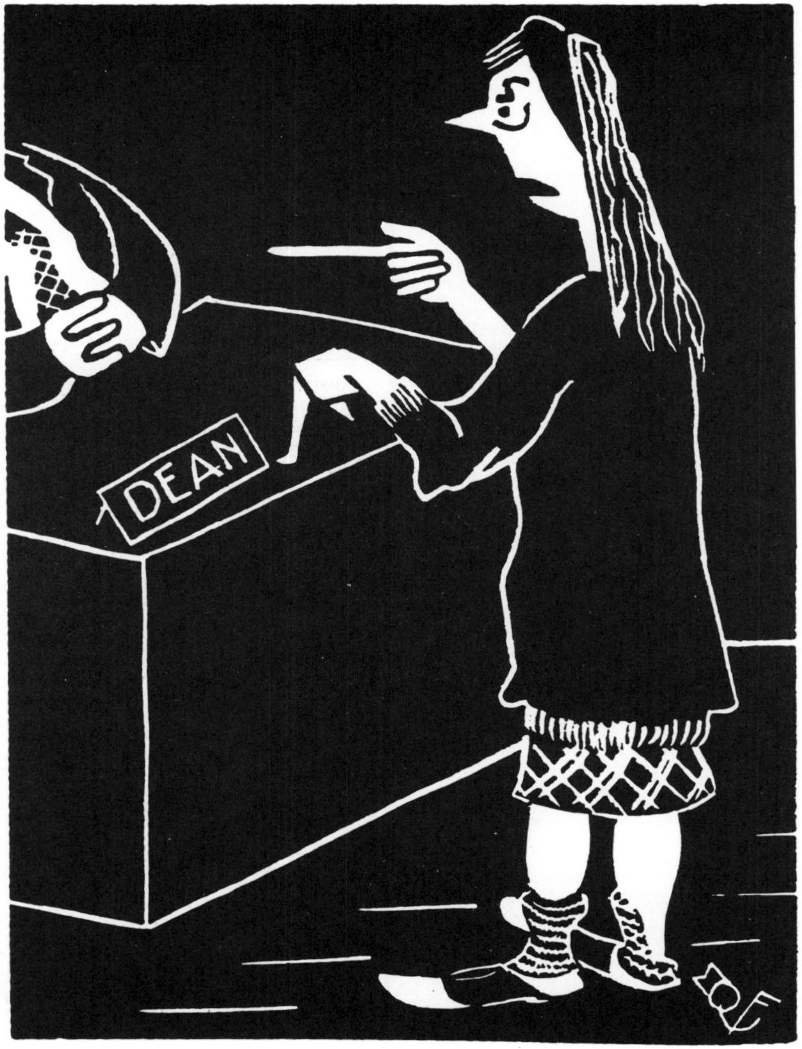
DEAN

"I demand an honorary organization for the C-Group!"

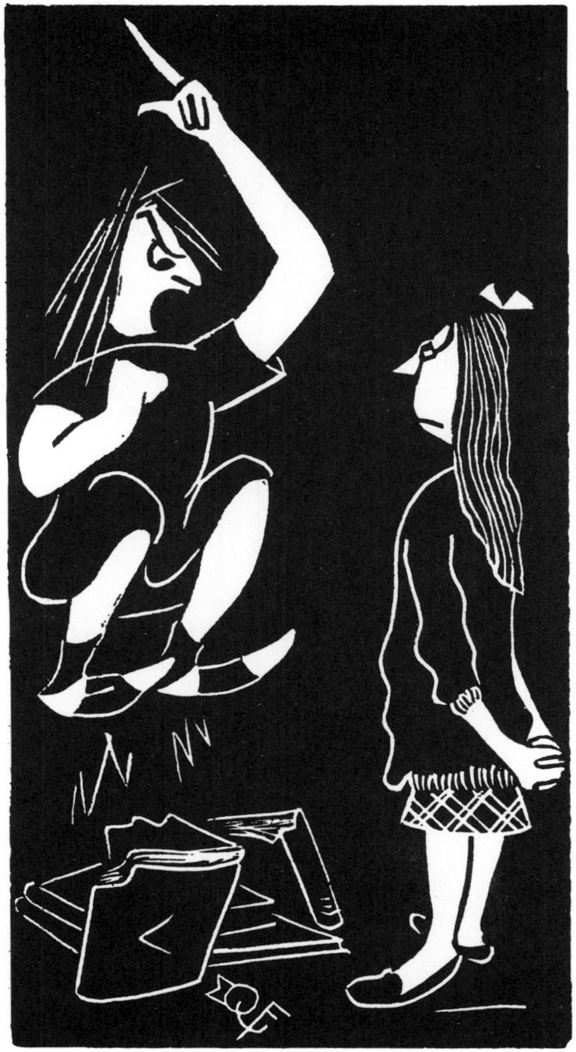

". . . and I ask you—how many Pilgrim Fathers had to write term papers during Thanksgiving."

"Do you have any books the faculty doesn't
particularly recommend?"

"I understand she says it's the happy way
of doing things."

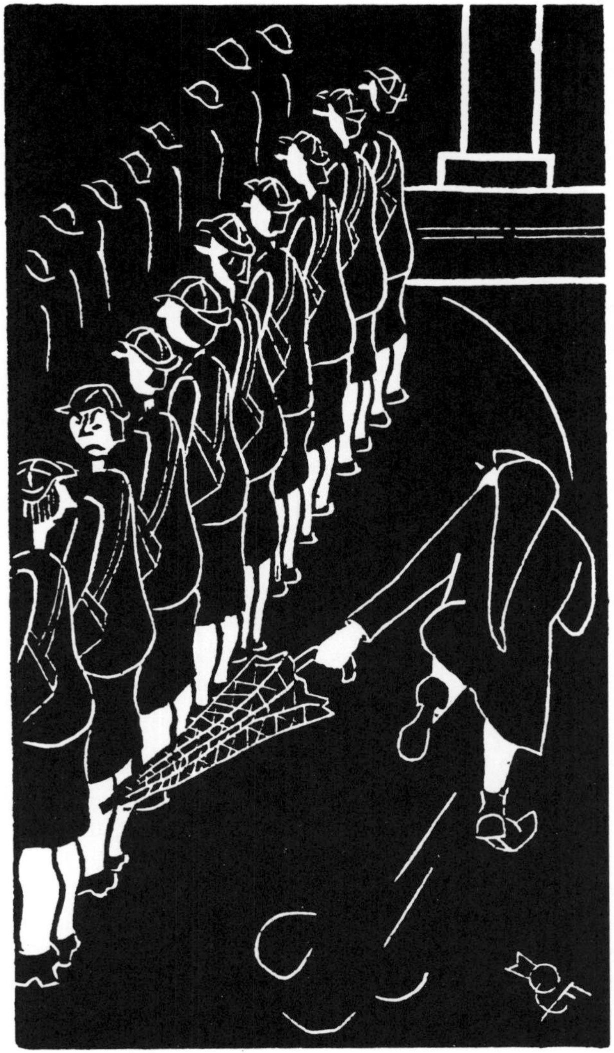

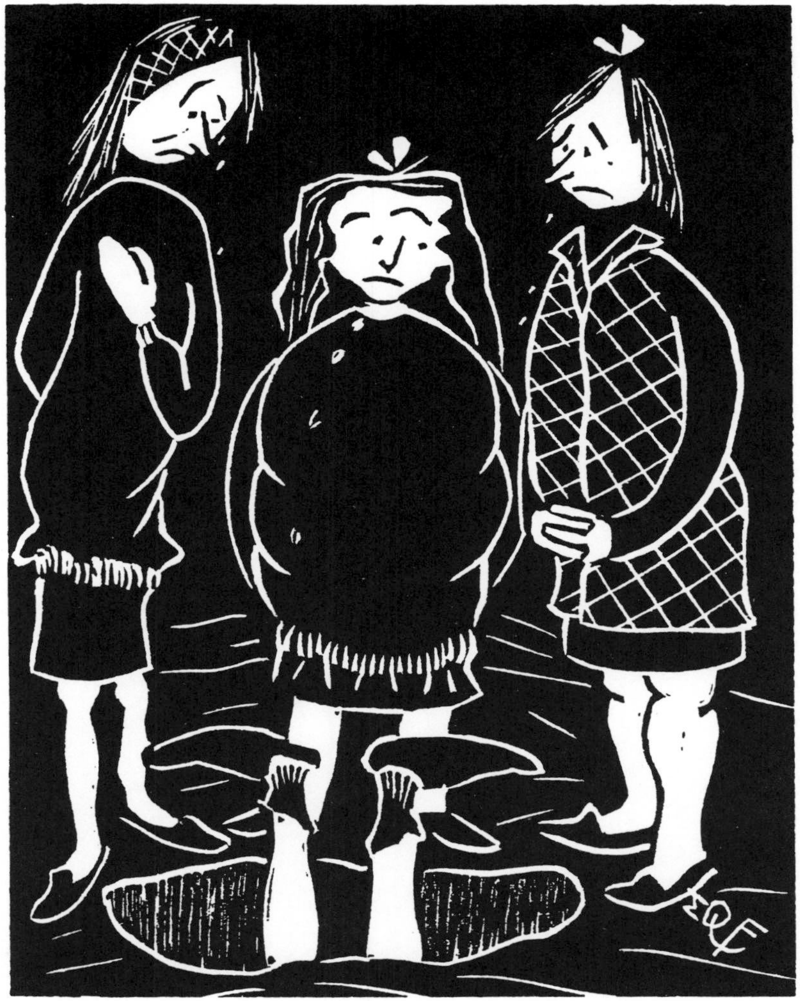

"She says we're on the threshold of social revolution."

"Hrump—not enough pride to build a nest!"

"Isn't it fortunate that Genevieve has completely
escaped that boy-crazy stage?"

"You don't mind if I get comfortable, do you?"

"Yeah, I know it's a nice shoe, lady, but it's not exactly what I'm looking for."

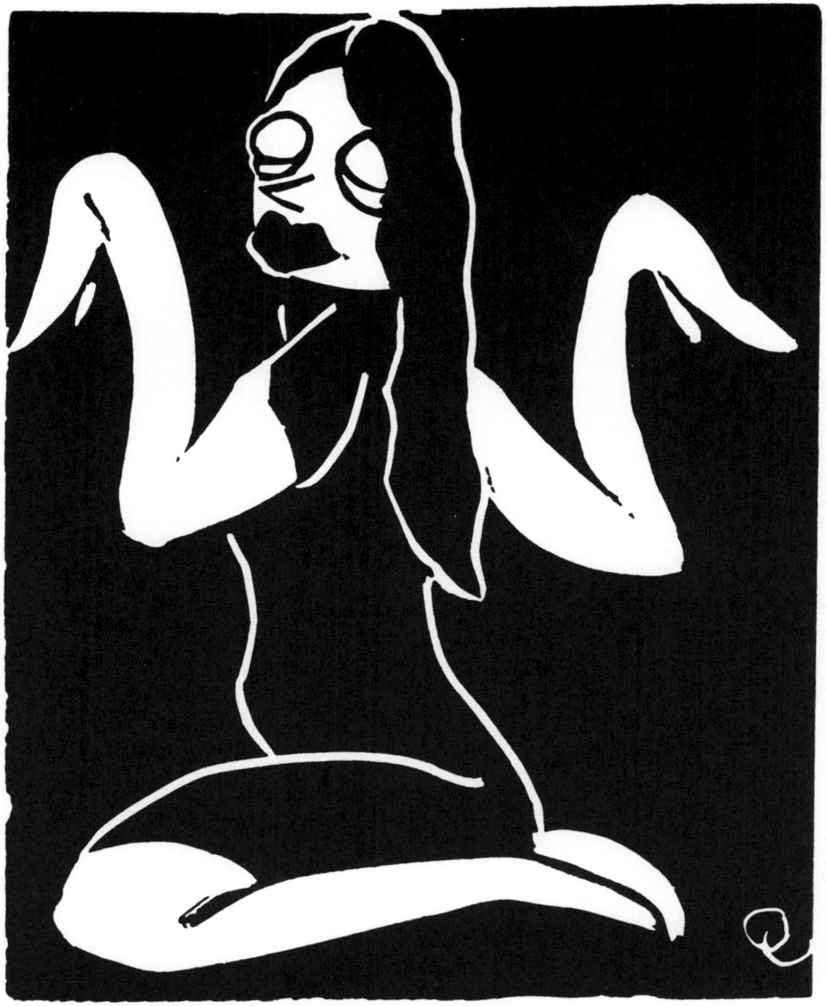

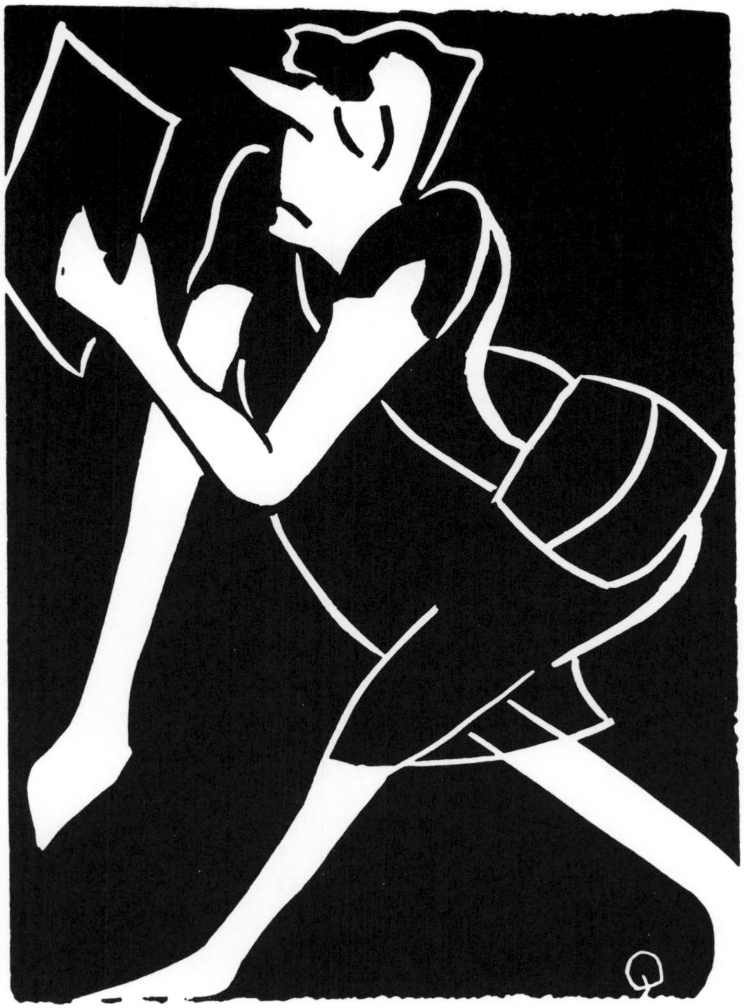

From *The Spectrum*   80 | 81

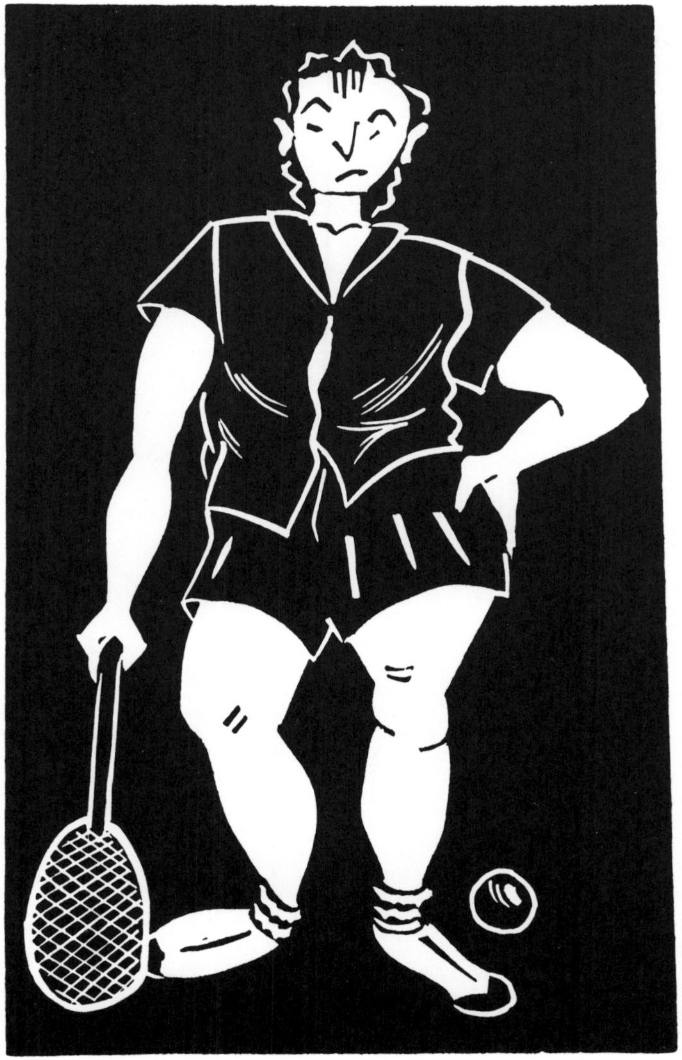

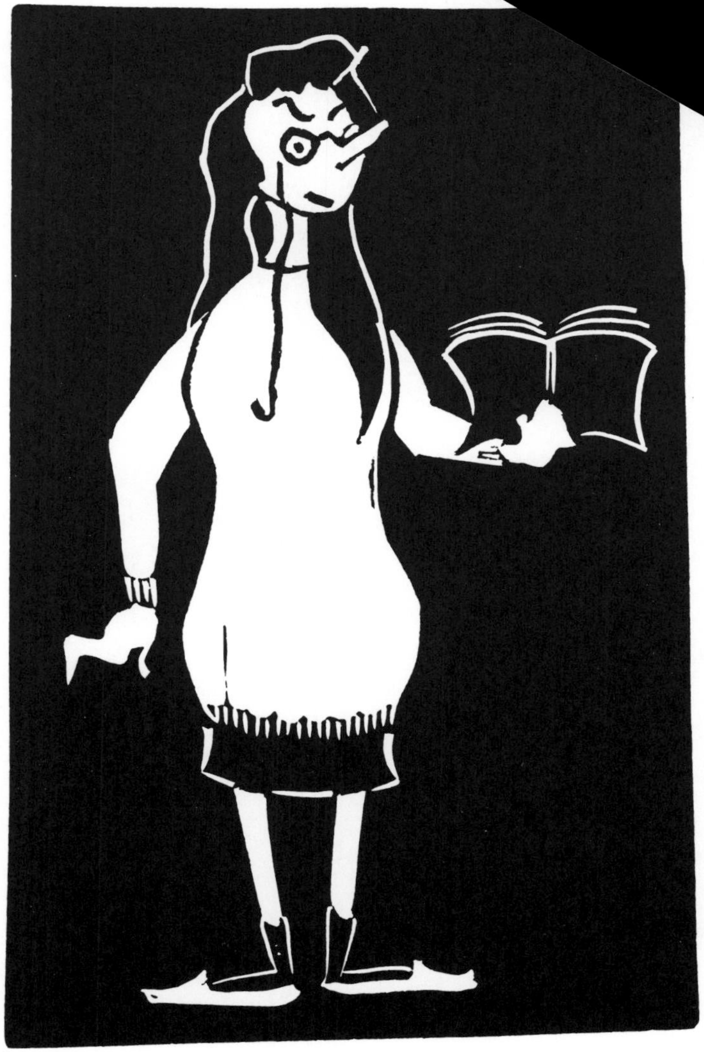

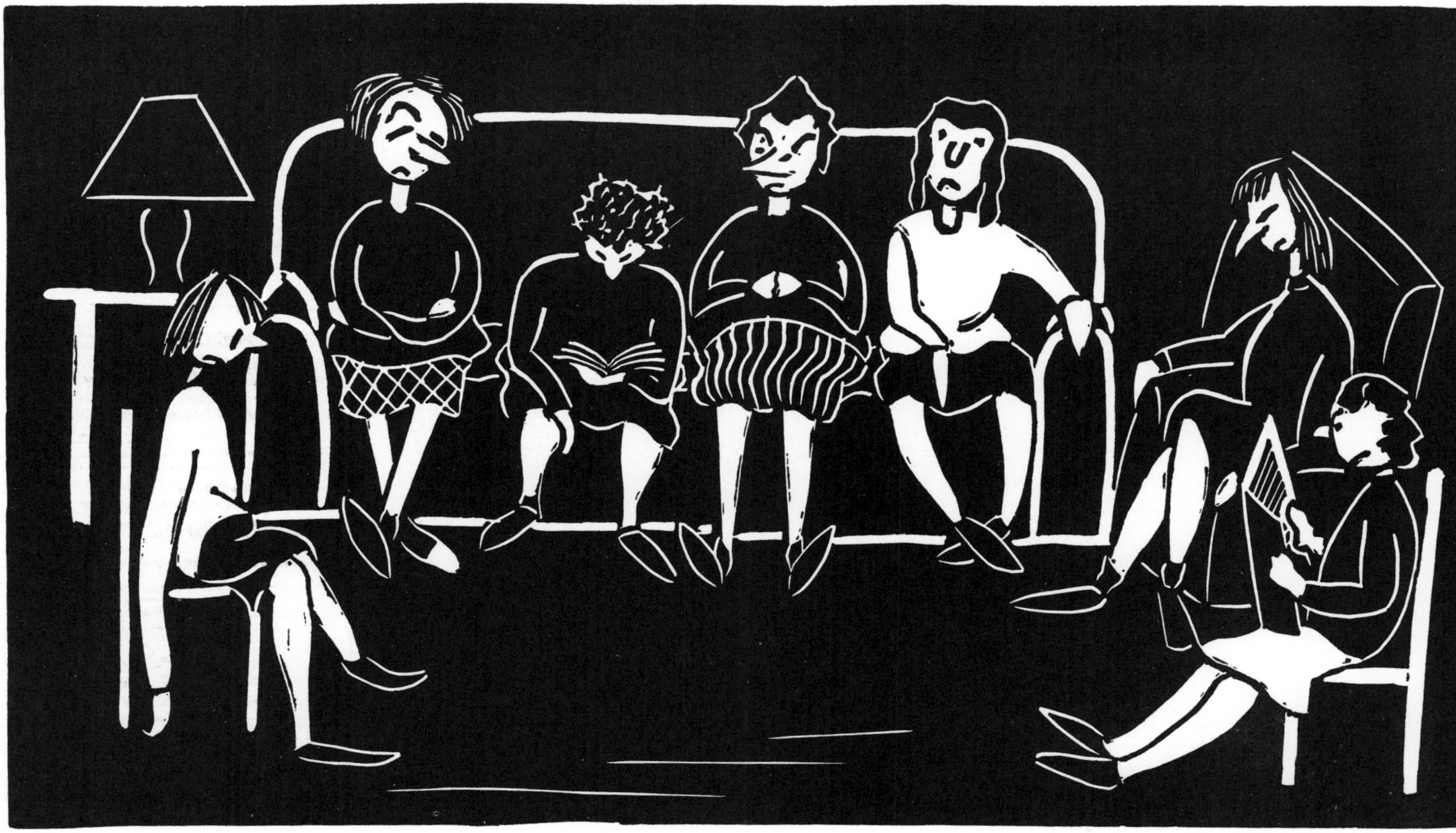

This Is Jessieville

They Guide Us on Our Way

Wayfarers

Our Naval Escort

We Learn To Lead

We Record Our Travels

Points of Interest

Having a Wonderful Time

Where Our Pennies Go

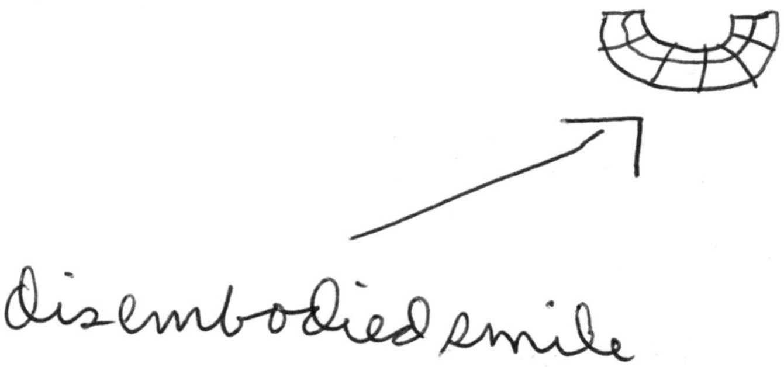
disembodied smile

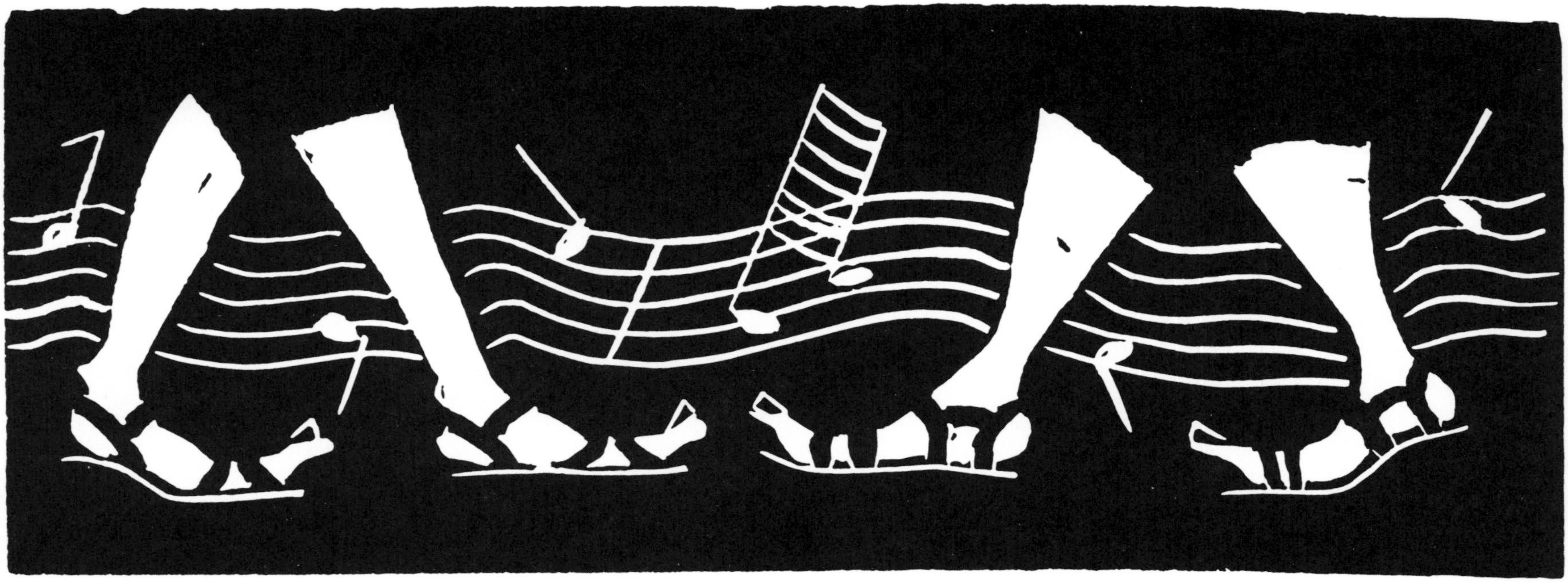

THE HABIT OF ART

BY **KELLY GERALD**

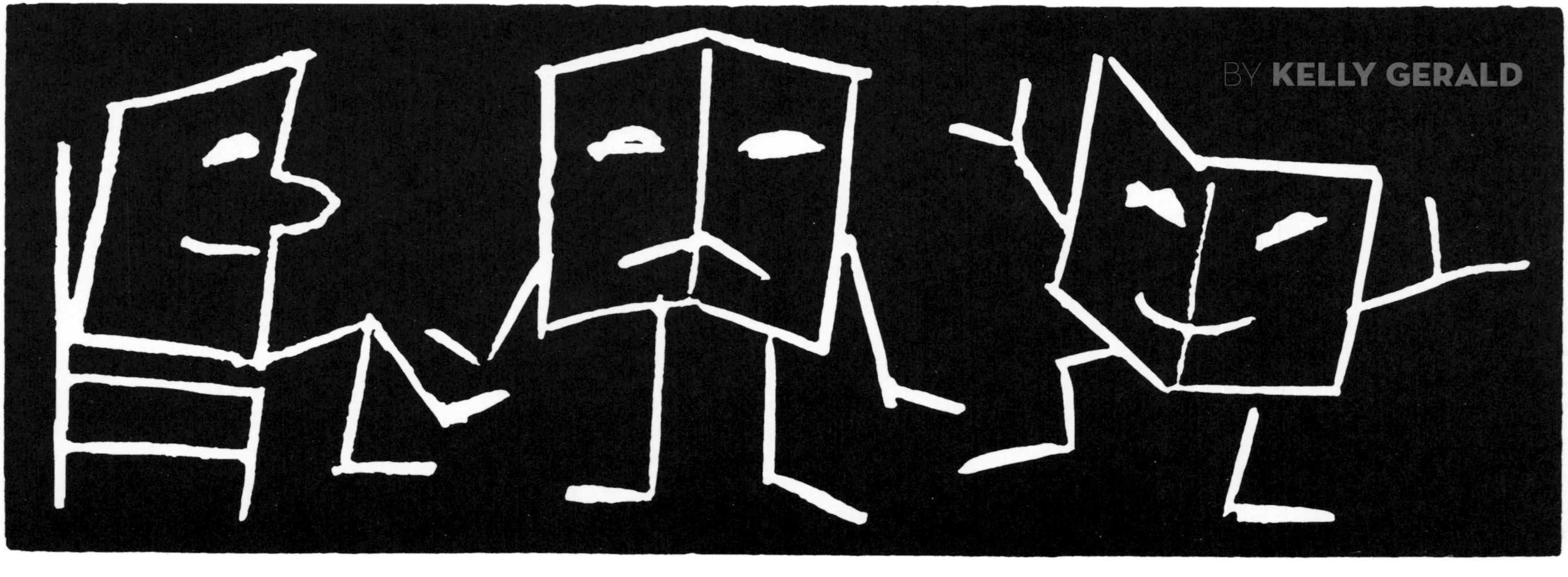

At the beginning of her career as a writer, Flannery O'Connor was diagnosed with lupus. She was twenty-five years old. She spent the last twelve and a half years of her life on her mother's farm in Milledgeville, in rural Georgia. It was from the house at Andalusia that she wrote the stories that made her famous. But she was no writerly recluse, and absolutely unsentimental about her illness. She presented nearly sixty lectures and readings during those years, traveling as far as Notre Dame in Indiana and Georgetown University in Washington, D.C.[1] A popular theme for these talks, naturally, was writing short stories.

If you were an aspiring writer at one of these lectures, what kind of advice could you expect to get? If you want to write fiction, stop looking for the right technique and just start *looking*.

"For the writer of fiction," she said, "everything has its testing point in the eye, and the eye is an organ that eventually involves the whole personality, and as much of the world as can be got into it."[2] This way of seeing she described as part of the "habit of art," a concept borrowed from the French Catholic philosopher Jacques Maritain. She used the expression to explain the way of seeing that the artist must cultivate, one that does not separate meaning from experience. And like any other habit, it has to be developed over time and through practice.

The visual arts became one of her favorite touchstones for explaining this process. Many disciplines could help your writing, she said, but especially drawing: "Anything that helps you to see. Anything that makes you look."[3] Why was this emphasis on seeing and vision so important to her in explaining how fiction works? Because she came to writing from a background in the visual arts, where everything that the artist communicates is apprehended, first, by the eye.

The habit of art was something she had developed on her own, long before she picked up the expression from Maritain and began to use it like a pointer in her talks. She had developed the habits of the artist, that way of seeing and observing and representing the world around her, from years of working as a cartoonist. She discovered for herself the nuances of practicing her craft in a medium that involved communicating with images and experimenting with the physical expressions of the body in carefully choreographed arrangements. Her natural proclivity for capturing the humorous character of real people and concrete situations, two rudimentary elements she later asserted form the genesis of any story, found expression in her prolific drawings and cartoons long before she began her career as a fiction writer.[4]

O'Connor's early work as a cartoonist remains a largely unacknowledged aspect of her creative life. From early childhood and throughout her adult years, she drew and painted. When she attended Peabody High School and Georgia State College for Women [GSCW] in Milledgeville, she created numerous cartoons and other illustrations for their student publications. These images comprise an independent and influential body that informs her work as a writer and is important to understanding the highly visual quality of her prose.

Beginning when she was very young, about age five, she drew and made cartoons, created small books, wrote stories and comical sketches, often accompanied by her own illustrations. Although her interest in writing was equally evident, O'Connor's talent as a cartoonist moved into the forefront by the time she reached high school. After her first cartoon was published in the fall of 1940, her work appeared in nearly every issue of her high school and college newspapers. When she graduated from GSCW in 1945, she was a celebrated local cartoonist preparing for a career in journalism that would, she hoped, combine work as a professional writer and a cartoonist.

That's the future she and everyone else envisioned for her when she left Milledgeville for graduate school at the University of Iowa. She had received a full scholarship to study journalism there, but her creative talents would soon take her in another direction.

Early in her first semester at Iowa, O'Connor visited Paul Engle, director of the Writers' Workshop, and shared with him what her brief

PREVIOUS SPREAD: In a chatty letter to Maryat Lee from May 1960, O'Connor encloses a photo of Lee's brother, GSCW President Robert E. "Buzz" Lee, that she had clipped from the local paper. After describing the occasion, a music recital, O'Connor added, "All that was lacking was you, padding around in your red sneakers and plaid pants." [Letter to Maryat Lee, May 1960, *Habit of Being*, 395.] She closes with the request "Keep me informed," followed by the drawing in place of her signature. Below it, she adds "disembodied smile" with an arrow to the drawing. [Unpublished portion of letter to Maryat Lee, May 1960. Special Collections, GCSU.]

OPPOSITE, TOP: *The Corinthian* (Spring 1943): 16. This decorative header appears above O'Connor's essay "Effervescence," a piece mocking the romantic gush that accompanied the arrival of spring at GSCW. According to biographer Brad Gooch, O'Connor's opening line, "Oh, what is so effervescent as a day in spring," parodies the line "And what is so rare as a day in June?" from the poem "The Vision of Sir Launfal" by James Russell Lowell. Edging toward the absurd, O'Connor burbles, "when we saw (what joyful sight) gross digits, brilliantly illuminated and protruding daintily from the apex of substantial little feet encased in seraphic footwear, we knew that frost was not expected again, and we rejoiced."

OPPOSITE, BOTTOM: *The Corinthian* (Spring 1943): 17. O'Connor's decorative header for the book reviews section repeats the theme of her previous version in the Winter 1943 issue. Two reviews by Elizabeth Andrews are published directly below, covering *The Human Comedy* by William Saroyan and *Blind Date with Mars* by Alice-Leone Moats.

time in the journalism program at Iowa had taught her: "I am not a journalist."[5] From that point forward, writing fiction became her focus. And her earlier work in the visual arts became an important foundation for her understanding of what stories are as she adapted her skills of observation and depiction, and her already polished sense of comedy, to work in prose.

— FROM CRAYONS TO CARTOONS —

Flannery O'Connor was born on March 25, 1925, in Savannah, Georgia, into a family of strong women presided over by her mother's relatives — a wealthy cousin Katie Semmes in Savannah and, from the Cline Mansion in Milledgeville, her mother Regina's older sister Mary, called "Sister" because she was the first girl born into the family after five boys.[6] People then knew her as "Mary" or sometimes, with a more Southern inflection, by her double name "Mary Flannery." Her parents, Regina and Edward O'Connor, showed every sign of devotion to their girl who was, as a friend of the family recalled, "beautifully cared for."[7]

Ties to the Irish Catholic community in O'Connor's family were strong, but it was her faith, not her Irishness, that came to characterize her sense of self and her place in the world. In both Savannah and Milledgeville, her relatives played a prominent role in church history. The first mass in Milledgeville was said in her great-grandfather's hotel room and, later, on the piano in his house.[8] In the Cathedral of St. John the Baptist in Savannah, across from O'Connor's childhood home on East Charlton Street, a large stained glass window is dedicated to the memory of Mary Ellen Flannery by her husband John Flannery, cousin Katie's parents. Her faith would become hugely important to her in her personal and her creative life as a fiction writer, though as a child, O'Connor recalled, its ritual observances were as natural to her as brushing her teeth.[9]

Up until the time she entered high school, O'Connor had a completely parochial education. In 1931, she enrolled at St. Vincent's Grammar School adjacent to the cathedral, but her mother moved her to Sacred Heart School across town when she was in the sixth grade. Almost immediately, beginning in her first grade year, O'Connor experienced conflicts with the nuns at St. Vincent's, a likely reason for the move to Sacred Heart. One of these early battles was about her attendance at a

RIGHT: O'Connor, early 1940s.

mandatory children's mass held in the basement of the cathedral. When her parents preferred to attend mass at a different time, their daughter had to account for her absence. Leonora Jones, who was in the first grade with O'Connor, remembers, "She'd stand there and tell sister, 'The Catholic Church does not dictate to my family what time I go to Mass.' I was five and she was six, and I knew she was different."[10]

An only child, O'Connor was shy and could be awkward with other children, and something of a brat who was used to having things go her way. In dealing with adults, she could be precocious and forward. According to one childhood friend, Newell Turner Parr, "she would say what she thought, which wasn't always acceptable."[11] She had a contrary, sometimes rebellious personality which came forward in creative and exasperating ways. She developed a problem with accepting authority. From early on, she called her parents by their first names, Regina and Ed.[12] She talked back to the nuns at school, irreverently substituted "Rover" for the name St. Cecilia in one of her writing assignments, brought castor oil sandwiches for lunch because she didn't like to share, popped the rubber bands off of her braces in class or caked them with peanut butter. She dipped snuff.[13]

Cleverness and mischief were certainly among her muses, but mostly she seemed inspired to keep to herself and spent much of her time alone in her room, drawing and writing stories. Her favorite subject? Birds. She loved drawing and making pictures, as most small children do, but as she grew, so did her talent and her ambition. A gift of crayons or drawing paper was more of a treat to her than being offered candy.[14] As time went by, her childhood drawings turned into illustrations for stories that she wrote, and these stories evolved into a series of small books dominated by her drawings. Her father played an important supporting role in stoking her artistic ambitions, showing off her talent and enjoying a little mischief himself. He taught her how to bind her books and had at least one of her manuscripts, a series of vignettes called "My Relitives," typed for her so that she could distribute it in style to said relatives.[15] O'Connor's satirical descriptions of her family members on that occasion caused a scandal that was remembered for decades. Retelling the incident more than forty years later, her mother recalled, "No one was spared."[16] It was an important lesson about how closely art should imitate life. Her cartoons later became notable for their ability to amuse her subjects without the sting.[17]

When, around 1931, she began to attend school and to learn the alphabet, O'Connor's drawings and her first attempts at representing language emerge together on the same piece of paper.[18] One of her earliest drawings combines letters and images on a section cut from the page of a child's primary school tablet. On one side of this small square of paper O'Connor made an early effort at writing — an E and a backward D for her father's name, among other unsteady letters at odd angles. Among these uneasily drafted capitals appears a half-formed face with large round eyes and dark, pronounced pupils. On the other side of the paper, O'Connor composed a complete drawing of what appears to be a turkey. A small stick figure with a smiling face and a tall hat soars overhead while the bird stands below, feet on the ground. She loved to turn things upside down and backward, a motif that shows up in her fiction as well as in her cartoons, like one she made when she was in college where one fish tells another, "You can go jump out of the lake."[19] These sorts of reversals became characteristic of her style.

This small drawing of a turkey may have been one of the tokens O'Connor hid under her father's plate at breakfast or inside his napkin as a special surprise.[20] Making a drawing or writing a bit of verse for him was an expression of affection and a way of soliciting his attention

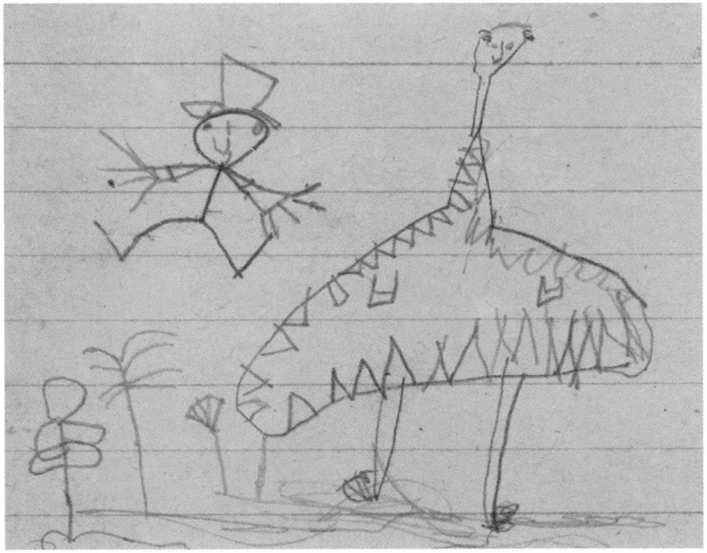

ABOVE: Untitled drawing, circa 1931. Pencil on ruled paper, 4 ¼ x 3 ¼ in. [Special Collections, GCSU.] This is likely one of the small drawings O'Connor used to make for her father, who would carry them around in his wallet to show off to people he met during the day.

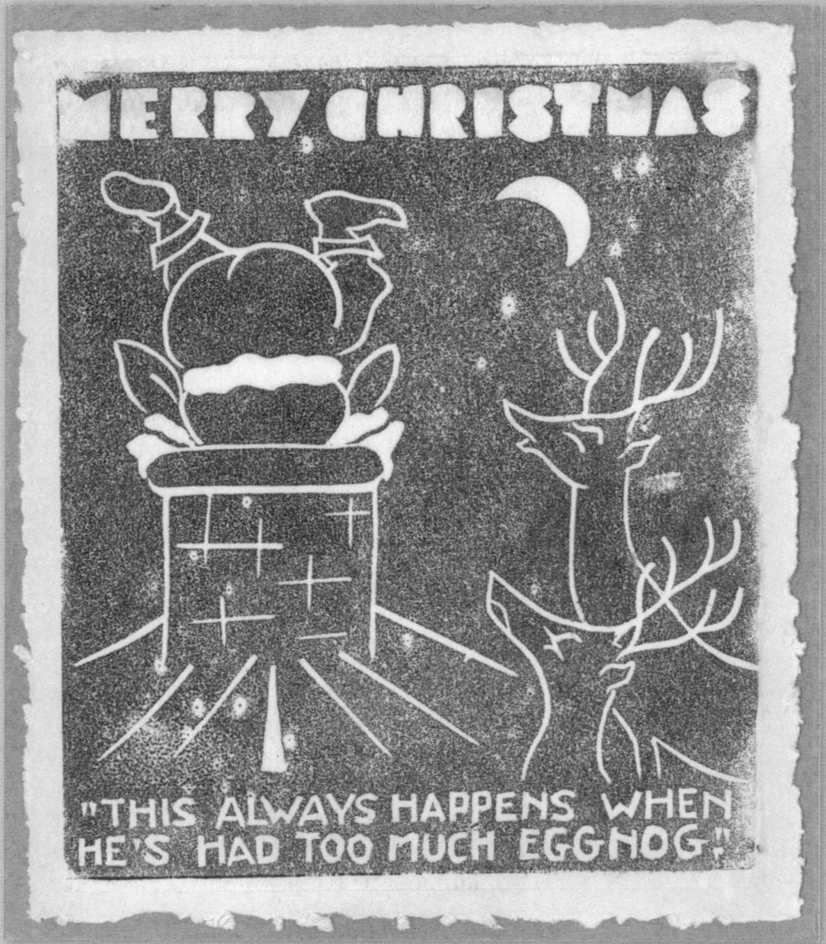
MERRY CHRISTMAS
"THIS ALWAYS HAPPENS WHEN HE'S HAD TOO MUCH EGGNOG!"

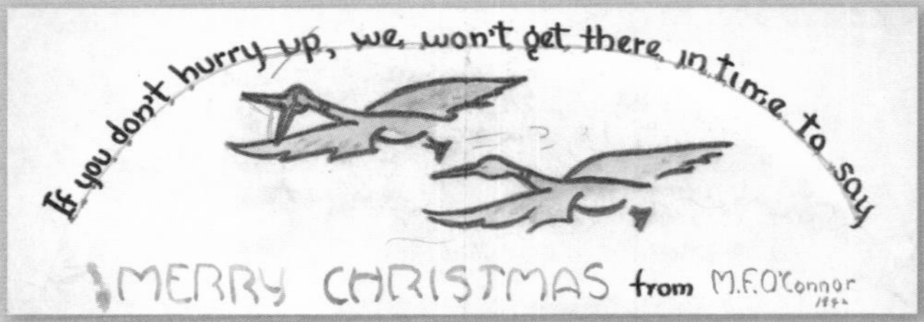
If you don't hurry up, we won't get there in time to say
MERRY CHRISTMAS from M.F.O'Connor

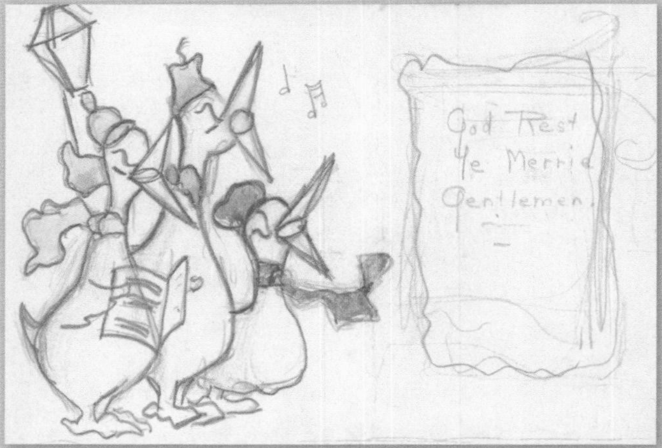
God Rest Ye Merrie Gentlemen.

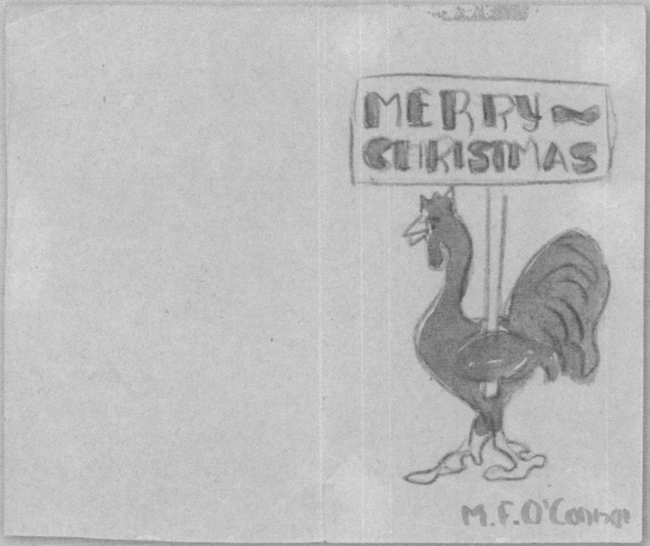
MERRY CHRISTMAS
M.F.O'Connor

CLOCKWISE FROM TOP LEFT: "This Always Happens When He's Had Too Much Eggnog," postmarked December 22, 1943. Original print from linoleum block cut on cotton paper backed with heavy construction paper, 4 ¼ x 5 ½ in. From the correspondence of Mary Virginia Harrison.; "If you don't hurry up, we won't get there in time to say Merry Christmas from M. F. O'Connor," 1942. Pencil, ink, and watercolor on construction paper. 12 ½ x 4 ¼ in.; "God Rest Ye Merrie Gentlemen," circa 1942. Pencil, crayon, and watercolor on construction paper. 4 x 4 in.; "Merry Christmas M. F. O'Connor," postmarked December 22, 1940. Pencil, crayon, and watercolor on brown paper, 5 x 6 in. [folded]. From the correspondence of Martha Pennington. [Special Collections, GCSU.]

and his praise. As most proud fathers share snapshots of their children, Ed O'Connor would sometimes fold these small drawings inside his wallet to show them off to people he met during the day.[21] Measuring about 4 ¼ x 3 ¼ inches, this little cartoon would have fit quite nicely inside a man's wallet.

The sense of play in their relationship is shown in another remarkable cartoon O'Connor made when she was about nine years old. Here she is walking down a street with her parents while Regina says, "Hold your head up, Mary Flannery, and you are just as bad, Ed." To which the child, who seems to be dragging along, sullenly replies, "I was readin where someone died of holding up their head."[22] The send up of her mother's nagging perfectionism and the daughter's sarcastic reply is intended to be relished by her fellow sloucher, her father. And like many of her other inventions, the drawing would have been made with his particular appreciation in mind.

Drawing may have been a refuge for her in a time of growing instability for the family as well. America's popular history is full of stories of good people enduring hard times during the Great Depression, relocating to find jobs and make a new start elsewhere, turning to extended family for support. The O'Connors' story is no different. Ed O'Connor's real estate business in Savannah had been in decline since the stock market crash in 1929 and the bottom fell out of the economy. In January 1938, after some heavy lobbying, he gained an appointment as senior zone real estate appraiser for the Federal Housing Administration in Atlanta. This began an unsettled period which eventually separated the family. They lived together for a time in Atlanta, but Regina and Flannery ultimately moved to Milledgeville, into the Cline Mansion with Regina's sister. Ed remained in Atlanta, as long as he was able to work.

By the fall of 1940, O'Connor was attending Peabody High School in Milledgeville.[23] The school was run by GSCW as part of a training program for teachers, and classes were held on the college campus, about a block from the Cline house. The first signs of her father's illness began to show shortly before the move to Atlanta. He had lupus, but it was kept private. It's unclear how much his daughter knew or when, but the severity of his illness could no longer be concealed after Ed returned to Milledgeville later that year. There was no effective treatment for lupus in those days; his physical decline was shocking and rapid. Ed O'Connor died on February 1, 1941, barely two months shy of his daughter's sixteenth birthday.

It was also in the fall of 1940 that O'Connor's mother contacted George Haslam, then a young professor at GSCW and the advisor for the student newspapers, both for the Peabody school and the college. Regina asked him if he could help get her daughter involved with the high school paper, since Mary Flannery was very shy and not likely to make the overture herself. O'Connor's mother also may have been looking for a project that would keep her daughter focused on something constructive during this difficult period for the family while providing an outlet for her drawing and writing. When Haslam asked the fifteen-year-old O'Connor if she would contribute something to *The Peabody Palladium*, she supposedly replied that she didn't know how to write, but she could draw.[24] This was the beginning of her career as a newspaper cartoonist.

She craved the recognition her drawings and stories brought her, and she used them to reach out to people as much as to sustain her introverted personality. In her later life, she admitted to a friend: "Needing people badly and not getting them may turn you in a creative direction, provided you have the other requirements."[25] Placing her work in the student paper was a way for a shy girl at a new school to find an audience, one that would appreciate her uniqueness and her talents. It also sparked an interest in publishing that put her on the path to becoming one of America's most celebrated fiction writers. Sharing her first published cartoons with her father during that fall and winter would have been a bright spot in an otherwise harrowing and uncertain time.

About a year later, in December of 1941, *The Peabody Palladium* published an article about O'Connor who was by that time one of the school's outstanding personalities. The short piece is titled "Peabodite Reveals Strange Hobby." What was the strange hobby? Collecting publishers' rejection slips. The article describes her ambitions to become a published writer and mentions the titles of three books: "Mistaken Identity," "Elmo," and "Gertrude." She bound them in pink cardboard and had a special box for each of them. One of her aunts reported that O'Connor was looking into having them copyrighted, with the help of an uncle in Atlanta.[26]

She had been writing and drawing since primary school, but her artistic interests were expanding. "Peabodite Reveals Strange Hobby" describes that she was also studying art and music, painting, and creating lapel pins that were being sold in a local drugstore. She was identifying herself as an artist and becoming known as one, but exactly want kind of artist and how far she would go, no one could guess. Her abilities as a cartoonist and illustrator, however, would take a front seat in the coming years.

O'Connor graduated from Peabody in the spring of 1942. She enrolled in her first college courses that summer, completing her degree at GSCW in three years as part of an accelerated wartime program. During those three years, her artwork came to dominate the college's publications, and she earned a reputation among the students and college alumnae as the "cartoon girl."[27] Between 1940 and 1945 O'Connor produced more than 100 cartoons and other images for the high school and the college's publications. Most of these images, and all of the cartoons for the student newspapers, were produced from linoleum block cuts.

In the fall of 1940, O'Connor became the art editor for *The Peabody Palladium*, shortly after she started submitting her cartoons for publication there. When she graduated from high school, her transition to GSCW and the role of cartoonist for the college paper barely interrupted the flow of her work. *The Colonnade* published her first cartoon in the fall of 1942. A few months later, in March 1943, she became the paper's art editor.

As her confidence grew and her cartoons became more widely celebrated, she eventually had a presence in all of GSCW's student publications. The college's literary journal, *The Corinthian*, had been publishing O'Connor's stories, satirical pieces, and poems since her freshman year. In her senior year, she was the journal's editor. *The Corinthian* became another showcase for her cartoons, including the covers for the fall 1944 and spring 1945 issues. Her cartoons also populated the pages of the GSCW yearbook, *The Spectrum*, for 1944 and 1945. The other staff members of the 1944 *Spectrum* gave her special recognition, publishing this acknowledgment for her in the yearbook: "Mary Flannery O'Connor, of cartoon fame, was the bright spot of our existence. There was always a smile in the *Spectrum* office on the days when her linoleum cuts came in."[28] During her senior year, she was *The Spectrum*'s feature editor, and her cartoons were the organizing principle of the entire design concept, providing a retrospective of O'Connor's years as the school's documentary cartoonist, caricaturist, and resident comic wit. The GSCW *Alumnae Journal* also picked up on her success, publishing her cartoons each year from 1942 till 1945.

Taken as a whole, O'Connor's cartoons comment on a predictable range of student experiences — the anticipation of vacations and holidays, complaints about teachers, cramming for final exams — and represent an impressive collection of single-frame satires anchored by human interaction. She targets the anti-intellectualism and social pretensions of her fellow students most frequently, but she also takes up some of the popular cranks about the school's shortcomings and responds to the effects of World War II upon the lives of the students, particularly the presence of the training school for WAVES that invaded the campus in early 1943. Her cartoons showed her talent for mimicking what she

Tuesday, December 16, 1941. THE PEABODY PALLADIUM

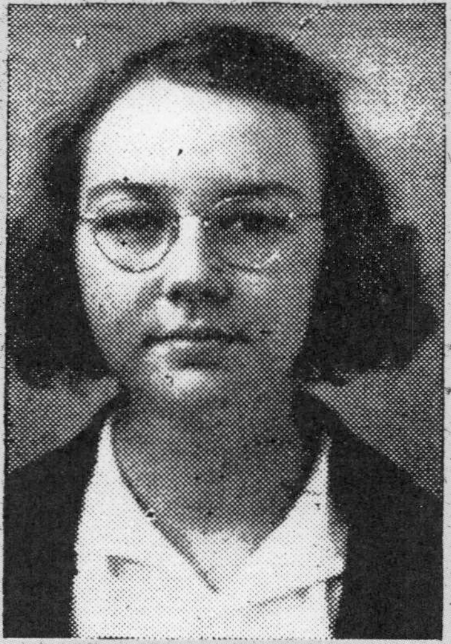

MARY FLANNERY O'CONNOR

Peabodite Reveals Strange Hobby

"Mary Flannery, what's your hobby?"

"Collecting rejection slips."

"What?"

"Publisher's rejection slips!"

And so the secret slipped out! Mary Flannery O'Connor is an author—of three whole books—illustrations and everything! But nothing can be put beyond Mary Flannery.—Nothing is impossible.

She began writing at the delicate age of six and just kept right on writing until "Mistaken Identity," "Elmo," and "Gertrude" were produced.

These, incidentally, are the same three books mentioned above. Each one of them is about a goose. They are of a novelty type—too old for young children and too young for older people.

As for Mary Flannery's ambition, she wants to keep right on writing, particularly satires.

One doesn't mention her without saying something about her pets. Herman is her remarkable gander who hatched out a brood of eight goslings. Mary Flannery brought him to school last summer and painted its portrait in art class. Hailie Selassie, her pet rooster, also served as a model.

Winston, a black crow, was added to her menageries when a neighbor shot the feathered rascal stealing pecans. Adolph, another rooster who roomed with Hailie, is now dead. His name was changed when neighbors began wondering about the "Here Adolph's!!" issued from Mary Flannery's back yard. Always there is an interesting collection of pets on the premises.

This Peabodite not only collects pets in the flesh, but also has a hundred and fifty replicas of them in china and glass.

And Mary Flannery is a musician. She plays a clarinet, accordian, and bull fiddle, "because," she says, referring to the latter, "I am the only one who can hold it up."

The cartoons in the Palladium by the art editor—Mary Flannery again—show the orginality and a keen sense of humor characteristic of the cartoonist. Cartoons, in fact, are right down her alley.

The note book which she has painted with oils and covered with cellophane is the envy of all Peabody. Recently, a collection of original lapel pins designed and executed by Mary Flannery were placed on sale at a local store.

A most unassuming person is Mary Flannery O'Connor, and clearly is one of Peabody's most outstanding personalities.

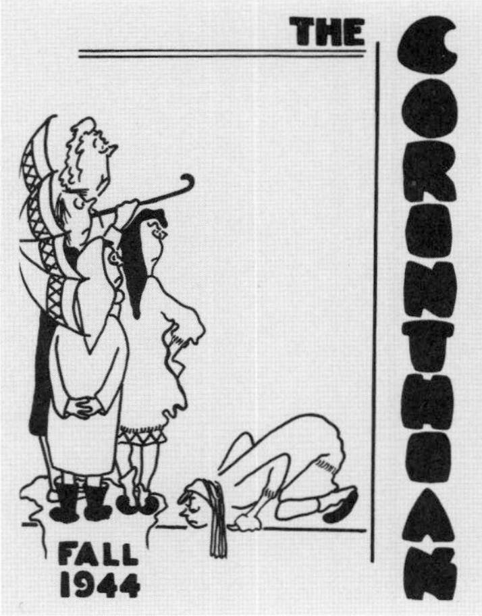
THE
CORINTHIAN
FALL
1944

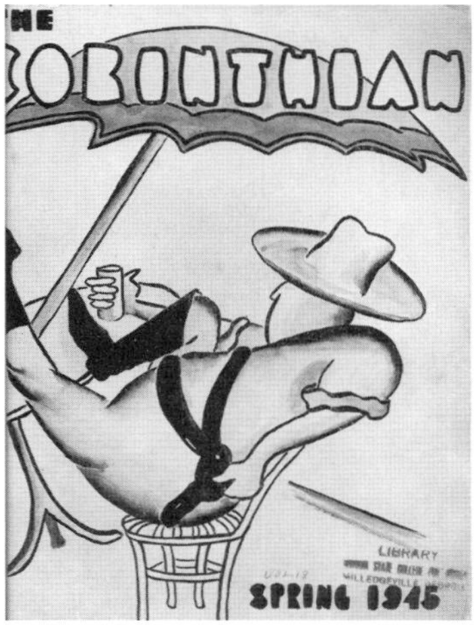
THE
CORINTHIAN
SPRING 1945

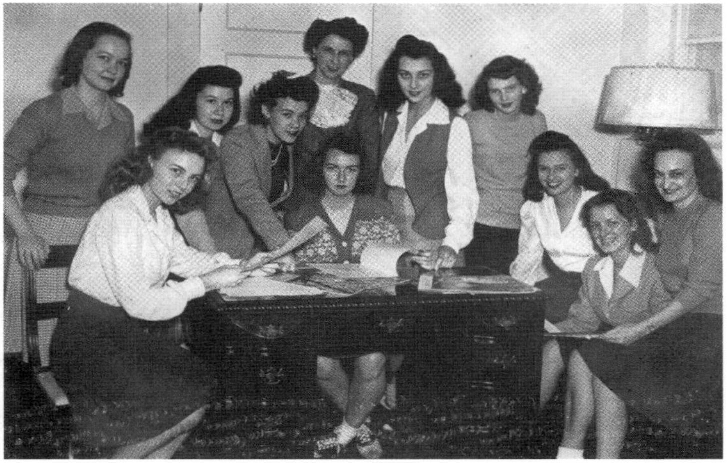

observed about people and their appearance, behavior, and manners, and what these things revealed about their character.

Her carefully drawn satires together with her use of recognizable scenes and landmarks from the campus give her work a documentary flavor, impressionistic but essentially revelatory and truthful. In her cartoons, O'Connor doesn't merely satirize student life, she created caricatures of her fellow students in which they could recognize themselves and, sometimes, portraits of the artist. And wherever O'Connor is, it's for sure one of her pets would not be far behind.

— A GIRL AND HER CHICKENS —

The birds that dominated O'Connor's childhood drawings remained an identifying feature of her humor during her high school and college years. In fact, they remained important to her for the rest of her life, and important to readers as a touchstone for understanding her delight in the absurd and her fascination with the grotesque.

When she was five years old, Pathé News came to Savannah to film her with her pet chickens. Rumor has it that O'Connor's cousin and benefactress Katie Semmes, also a bird lover, had arranged the visit, or had at least solicited Pathé's attention. Like an early version of YouTube, Pathé's short films were about real people and had a popular appeal; they ran before the feature film in theaters as part of the entertainment. Pathé didn't send a cameraman all the way to Georgia just to film a little girl with her chickens. O'Connor had something exotic to offer that attracted their attention — a buff Cochin Bantam that she had trained to walk backward. The short film, shown in theaters about two years later, was titled "Unique Chicken Goes in Reverse."

As an adult, O'Connor sometimes retold the story in a self-mocking way as the high point in her life[29] and credited Pathé News with sparking the obsession with birds that led her to raise peacocks, another kind of unique chicken. "From that day with the Pathé man I began to collect chickens," O'Connor wrote in a 1961 *Holiday* magazine article. "I had to have more and more chickens."[30] And she was attracted most to the ones that were different in some way, or suitable for the pages of *Ripley's Believe It or Not.*[31]

ABOVE, FAR LEFT: Cover illustration. *The Corinthian*, Fall 1944. An editor's note published on page three describes the artist's objective: "Had the cover-girls realized that they were being recorded, they would have undoubtedly draped themselves to better personal advantage; but when we caught them examining our cover so critically, we couldn't resist making them a part of it. So that we won't discredit them too much, we'll admit that a less biased investigation might not show them with as many obtuse angles."

ABOVE, LEFT: Cover illustration. *The Corinthian*, Spring 1945. O'Connor, who served as the editor for this issue of *The Corinthian*, explains the allegorical meaning of her cover art in a note published on page three: "The dashing young man on the cover represents Spring at G.S.C.W. He is also a symbol for the spirit of vitality, the eagerness for education, and the alertness to world problems — qualities which are so evident on our campus at this particular season."

ABOVE: O'Connor (center) with the staff of *The Corinthian*, 1945.

In 1956, she described her childhood fixation in a letter to her friend Betty Hester: "I drew — mostly chickens, beginning at the tail, the same chicken over and over beginning at the tail."[32] When she was about ten years old, she formed a club called the Merriweather Girls, borrowing the name from the popular 1930s adventure books by Lizette Edholm. They met at O'Connor's house, where their self-appointed president would read to them from her stories about a family of ducks traveling the world; illustrated with her own drawings, of course.[33] Her enthusiasm carried over into her work for school, leading one exasperated nun to sputter that she never wanted to hear about another duck or chicken.[34]

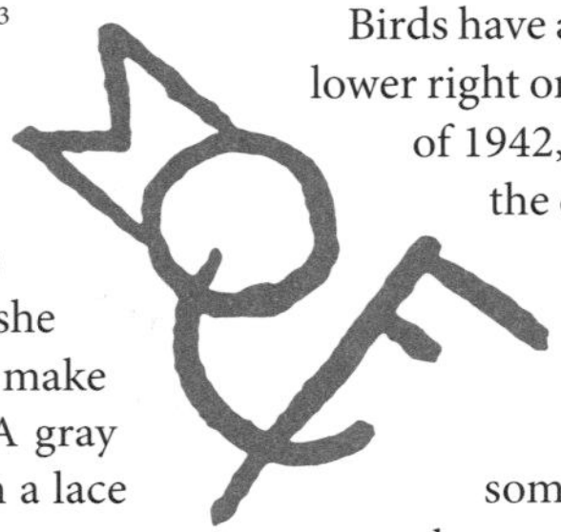

Borrowing a page from Beatrix Potter, she began to dress up her animal friends, suitable for the more human roles she imagined for them. "I could sew after a fashion and I began to make clothes for chickens," she wrote in "The King of the Birds." "A gray bantam named Colonel Eggbert wore a white piqué coat with a lace collar and two buttons in the back."[35] Members of her Girl Scout troop in Milledgeville, Regina Sullivan and her sisters, recall that O'Connor would bring her pet chicken Aloisius to meetings, providing them all with an entertaining spectacle: "He was dressed in his little gray shorts, a little white shirt, a jacket, and a red bow tie."[36]

Years later, comparing notes with Betty Hester over their childhood reading habits, they discovered that neither of them could stand *Alice in Wonderland*. She confessed that she also found *Pinocchio* terrifying. "I was always a *Peter Rabbit* man myself," she wrote.[37] Her taste for making up stories about the adventures of animals and her drawings of birds share similarities with Potter's illustrations, including the clothes. Like Potter, she gave her animal companions a special status, populating the landscape of her imagination with them instead of people. In a story O'Connor wrote for a creative writing class in high school, she describes a girl's deep emotional attachment to a pet rooster named Sillow that she loves like a "sibling."[38] When it is killed, she tries to keep the carcass in her room. O'Connor biographer Jean Cash observes that the bird in this story seems to be the girl's only source of emotional warmth.[39]

O'Connor never quite breaks off the obsession with birds. It's hard to read any story of hers without noticing a chicken or a peacock walking through it. In "The Life You Save May Be Your Own" the moon roosts in a fig tree with the chickens, and the younger Lucy Nell Crater's eyes are "as blue as a peacock's neck."[40] In "Parker's Back" the only one of Parker's tattoos that his wife admires looks like a chicken.[41] In "The Displaced Person" the peacocks on Mrs. McIntyre's farm draw the gaze of the priest, and in the workers' quarters she prepares for the Guizacs, the flowered curtains are made from chicken feed sacks.[42] A peacock's tail unfurls in the night sky above Tarwater in *The Violent Bear It Away*, dotting the heavens with "fixed tranquil eyes like the spread tail of some celestial night bird."[43] And in "The Enduring Chill" the stain on the ceiling that looks like a "fierce bird" descends as the Holy Ghost to Asbury's bed.[44]

Birds have a place in O'Connor's cartoon world as well, usually in the lower right or left corner of a cartoon as the artist's signature. In the fall of 1942, when she began to publish some of her satirical pieces in the college literary journal, *The Corinthian*, she signed herself "M. F. O'Connor,"[45] echoing her father's use of initials in his signature, "E. F. O'Connor."[46] When signing her cartoons, O'Connor transformed her initials into a playful stamp of her identity. She experimented with some variations, sometimes imitating a copyright symbol, but settled primarily on a rearrangement of her initials, M. F. O. C., into a monogram, or pictogram, that looked like a bird with the "M." for an open beak, the "O." as the head, the "C." as the body, and "F." forming the foot and wing. This is how she signed her first cartoon for the GSCW newspaper, *The Colonnade*, in October 1942, and most of those that followed.

The signature is distinctive, but it wasn't completely her own invention. This kind of monogram art was a pop culture trend and is documented in a Paramount Pictures newsreel, "Unusual Occupations," dating to World War II.[47] Like a kind of personal heraldry, each monogram was designed to represent the individual's favorite hobby or profession. A young man in the Navy, for instance, could have the initials for his name and rank rearranged into the shape of an anchor, and so on. These monogram images were used to adorn stationary, handkerchiefs, business cards, and other personal items. O'Connor's monogram may have looked like a bird, observed her college friend Betty Boyd Love, "but I'm sure she would have said it was a chicken."[48]

O'Connor's bird signature provided an ingenious way of signing her work. It also was an expression of that most sought-after of possessions, another unique chicken. It was not merely a way of branding the cartoon with her initials, but a way of projecting herself into the scene, since her name and the bird image are communicated by the same sign. The artist certainly appears to be aware that her quirky obsession also made her something of a unique chicken, too, indicating another source of her humor — self-satire.

She included representations of herself in her cartoons in other ways as well, sometimes in the form of more conventionally styled self-portraits. These cartoons show what fans of her collected correspondence in *The Habit of Being* have long enjoyed about her personality — that she was always willing to write herself into a comic scene.

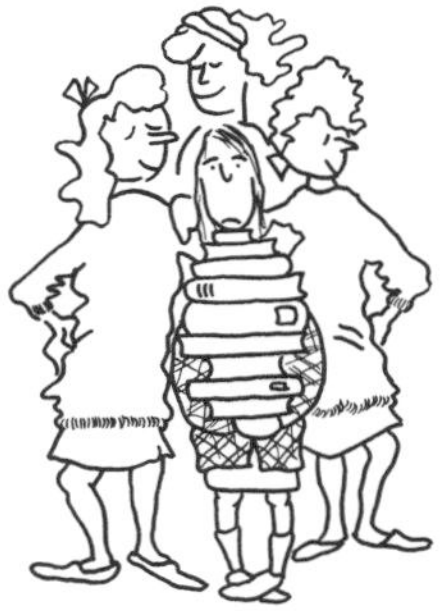

Betty Boyd Love, who was perhaps her closest friend at the time, describes "Wayfarers" from the 1945 *Spectrum* as her favorite cartoon. The "harried-looking limp-haired 'studious' type, staggering under a huge stack of books," she explained, was "probably meant to be Flannery herself." [49] She was often seen walking on campus carrying a large stack of books.

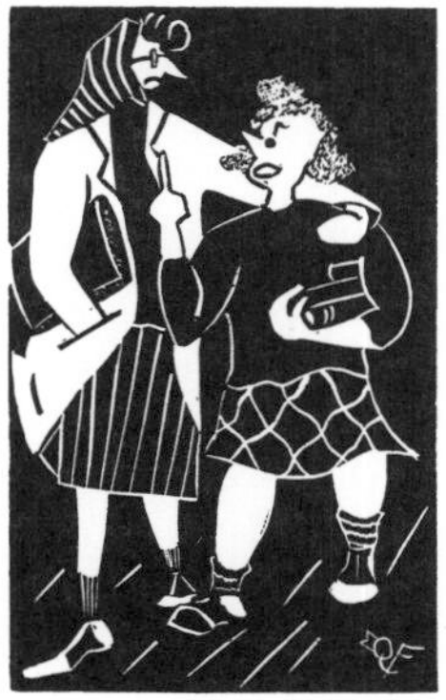

Other cartoon figures resemble O'Connor, mimicking her physical appearance and details from her life. In the January 9, 1943, *Colonnade* cartoon "Aw, don't worry about not getting on the Dean's List. It's no fun going to the picture show at night anyway," the tall lanky girl on the left with the dark hair and glasses, carrying a large book tucked under her arm, has an O'Connor-like appearance, but the Dean's List published on the front page of that issue has another punch line. O'Connor's name wasn't on it. During her years at GSCW, this was the only time she didn't make the Dean's List. And what was playing in the local theaters that week? Pictures starring silver screen heartthrobs Errol Flynn and Tyrone Power. Truly no fun at all.

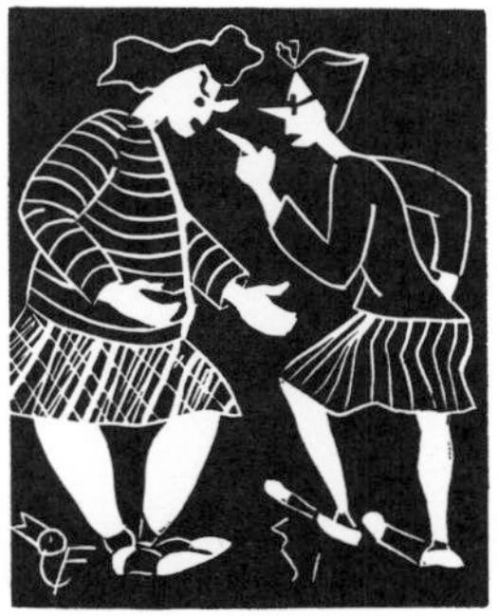

An O'Connor-like girl with glasses also appears in the January 30, 1943, *Colonnade* cartoon "But I tell you, you don't have to get a rooster to tell when to get up; all you have to do is set your clock back." This time she's vigorously defending the benefits of owning poultry while her fellow student appeals for a less extreme solution. Front page news in this issue: "College Sets Clocks Back," an article about the school's decision to change from Eastern Standard War time to Central Standard War time.[50] Happy to be the butt of her own joke, who else besides O'Connor would think you need a rooster to get up early enough to get to class?

One of O'Connor's classmates, Hazel Smith Ogletree, believed that O'Connor "patterned her cartoons after an exaggerated physical picture of herself." "She could make us all look like her," Oglegree said, "yet keep our own special identity."[51] The cartoonist's special identity, however, continues to break the surface here and there. "I remember sitting on the swing on the front porch of Greene Street, and Flannery walking by with this little bantam on a leash," said a cousin, Frances Florencourt, describing her earliest memory of O'Connor. Perhaps her cousin wasn't the only one watching. The girl with a pet bird on a leash shows up again in a Thanksgiving cartoon, "Just the thought of getting away from here for a few days unhinges some people, you know," from the November 23, 1943, issue of *The Colonnade*. In this incarnation, a GSCW student walks by with a huge turkey on a lead, while another girl taking in the bizarre scene with a friend makes the sideways remark.

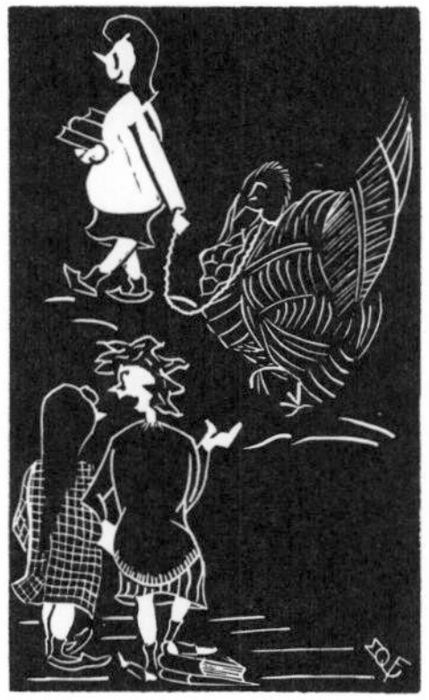

A favorite self-satirizing cartoon singled out by O'Connor biographers Jean Cash and Brad Gooch appears in the April 3, 1943, issue of *The Colonnade.*[52] A small girl in glasses sits alone on the side of a crowded dance floor, evidently passed over by the boys. With a grin, she remarks confidentially to the viewer, "Oh, well, I can always be a Ph.D." Gooch in particular comments on this image as a representation of O'Connor, connecting it to her short-lived relationship with a young Marine sergeant, John Sullivan. They attended a college dance, but only one. Gooch writes that Sullivan "quickly discovered she was a truly bad dancer."[53] Yes, she may have had a "tin leg,"[54] as she admitted to a friend years later, but she was also a very serious-minded girl with substantial ambitions. Before she left GSCW, she completed the education requirements that would have qualified her to teach high

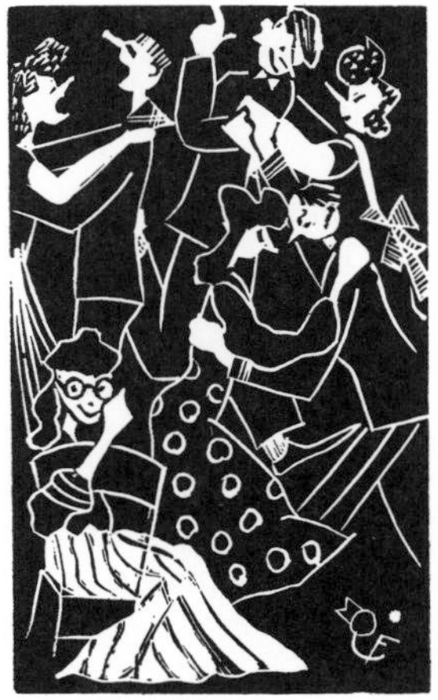

school, but she did everything within her power to prevent that fall-back position from becoming her future. As she phrased it in an autobiography written at Iowa, she didn't want to get stuck teaching ninth graders in "Podunk, Georgia."[55]

O'Connor got a headline and her photo in the local paper at the end of her freshman year when a Georgia poet and former music teacher at GSCW, Nelle Womack Hines, wrote about her for the *Macon Telegraph and News*. "Mary O'Connor Shows Talent as Cartoonist" appeared on page three of the Sunday paper, June 13, 1943.

Among the observations about O'Connor's work devoted to the adventures of her feathered friends, Hines points to one of the most distinctive features of O'Connor's cartoons, her buddy comedy routine: "Mary presents two students in her cartoons — a tall and lanky 'dumb bunny' and a short and stocky 'smart-aleck' — female of course."[56] Not all of O'Connor's incarnations of her duo follow this formula, sometimes it's the tall girl who gets off the zinger or stares with an irritated expression at some remark made by her friend, but the pattern is there. A tall one and a short one, a thin one and a chubby one, a smart one and a dumb one, and it's their remarks, sour expressions, and wise-cracking exchanges that form the pattern of many of her jokes.

— BUDDY COMEDY —

The strong tradition of buddy comedy in the popular media of the 1930s and '40s appears to have influenced O'Connor's narrative style and choice of characters. One could even call this era the golden age of the comedy duo. Jack Benny and Eddie Anderson's routines on Benny's radio programs during these decades made him and sidekick Rochester household names. George Burns and Gracie Allen rose to prominence in radio in the mid 1930s, and their show garnered top ratings on NBC and CBS before transitioning *The Burns and Allen Show* to television in 1950, where it ran for another eight years. During the 1940 election year, their program's running gag "Gracie Allen for President" was popular enough that listeners voted for Allen as a write-in candidate on election day. Bud Abbot and Lou Costello became box office stars with their 1941 film *Buck Privates*. A year earlier, their famous "Who's on First?" routine was first seen by movie audiences in *One Night in the Tropics*. At the most essential level, each team follows a recognizable pattern — a pair of contrasting physical types, one smart or playing straight for his partner and the other a "dumb bunny," engaged in a routine of cleverly contrived punch lines and dialogue that flirted with the absurd.

MARY FLANNERY O'CONNOR

Mary O'Connor Shows Talent As Cartoonist

By NELLE WOMACK HINES

Mary Flannery O'Connor, who has just completed her freshman year at the Georgia State College for Women in Milledgeville, is fast making a name for herself as an up-and-coming cartoonist. A female Ogden Nash, Mary not only draws her pictures and writes her captions, but goes Ogden one better by carving her own cuts on a linoleum block.

This young artist, the 17-year-old daughter of Mrs. Edward F. O'Connor Jr., is a Milledgeville girl and doesn't remember the day when she wasn't writing and illustrating humorous verse. During pre-college days at Peabody High of GSCW, her cartoons and writings appeared in that school paper. When Mary became a freshman, she was drafted by the Colonnade, the GSCW weekly, which carries one of her cartoons in each issue. She fashions a bird from her initials—MFO—with which she signs all cartoons.

When asked how she went about her work, Miss O'Connor replied that first—she caught her "rabbit." In this case, she explained, the "rabbit" was a good idea, which must tie up with some current event or a recent happening on the campus. Usually, Mary presents two students in her cartoons—a tall and lanky "dumb-bunny" and a short and stocky "smart-aleck"—female, of course. A keen sense of humor enables her to see the funny side of situations which she portrays—minus a sting. The appearance of several hundred WAVES on the campus of GSCW during the early spring gave new impetus to this freshman's talent and some of her cleverest cartoons have dealt with the WAVE situation.

Miss O'Connor's scrap books are most interesting. One booklet, bound and illustrated in color by herself, bears the title "Mistaken Identity," and contains the story of Herman, the Duck, told in verse. The foreword reads: "The following is a drama especially prepared for highly intelligent adults and precocious children." The lines quoted below are but a part of the whole "drama," but tell a tale.

"Now Herman was a happy duck
   for he enjoyed life,
Until we thought it would be
   nice if he could have a wife.
And so, we bought him three of
   them, they all were perfect
   ladies—
But Herman took one look and
   honked, 'You gals can go to
   Hades!'
And then one day I saw the light
   —the truth down to a dreg—
For the point of the story came
   to me when Herman laid an
   egg.'"

Miss O'Connor frankly states that her literary ambition is to be able to write prose satire. She plans to work hard and hopes some day to find a place where her satiric essays and cartoons will fit to good advantage. Mary makes the dean's list and much of her work, both cartoon and essay, has appeared not only in the Colonnade, but in the Corinthian, GSCW Literary quarterly, and the Alumnae magazine.

The archetypal comedy duo of the age, of course, was Stan Laurel and Oliver Hardy. They set the standard by which all other buddy acts that followed them would be measured, in the way that all Southern writers are inevitably compared to William Faulkner. The team gained popular acclaim in the 1920s in a series of comedies produced by Hal Roach. Unlike many actors of their generation, they survived the transition to sound in the '30s with a style of dialogue that complemented the visual comedy that had fueled their success in silent films.

One lean and awkward, the other heavy and moon-faced, their contrasting physiques helped to exaggerate their appearance to the level of caricature. Another hallmark of their style was the constant erosion of Hardy's pretense to intelligence and sophistication by his companion's simpleminded buffoonery. Similar to the college students portrayed in O'Connor's cartoons, the characters Laurel and Hardy created were not so much adults as they were children playing at being adults, with their foibles and shortcomings in those roles the source of much of their comedy. Considered against this background, some of the comical pairs O'Connor created in her fiction bear similarities to these child-like characters, perpetually marginalized and struggling along in a world of sophistication that is beyond their ability to fully enter, like Hazel Motes and Enoch Emory in *Wise Blood*, Mr. Head and Nelson in "The Artificial Nigger."

O'Connor's tall, lanky "dumb bunny" and short, stocky "smart aleck" show that she had taken up a formula for two-person comedy found in some of the most popular radio programs and films of her time. But she may have had a special reason to attend to the humor of Laurel and Hardy: Oliver Hardy grew up in Milledgeville. Her aunt Katie Cline, nicknamed "Duchess" supposedly because of her resemblance to illustrator John Tenniel's Duchess in *Alice in Wonderland*,[57] was a member of the Georgia Military College Players Club and performed in light comedies with Bardy, Oliver Hardy's brother.[58] O'Connor and her mother were living with her aunts Katie and Mary, and a great aunt, Gertie, while O'Connor attended high school and college in Milledgeville. It seems improbable that her aunt's connection to one of the most famous films stars of all time would have gone without, at least, an occasional remark.

"Ollie" was born Norvell Hardy in 1892. His mother, Emily, ran the Baldwin Hotel in Milledgeville after the death of her husband, Oliver. Similar to O'Connor, he later adopted a different name for himself, his father's name, which became the one the public recognizes. Emily enrolled her unruly teenaged son in Georgia Military College, as much for the discipline as for the physical improvement she thought he needed (at

fourteen, he weighed 250 pounds).[59] He was enthralled with the entertainers and theater troupes that stayed in the hotel, and gained a reputation as a singer and a natural comedian in his youth. "Back home he was always asked to umpire the local baseball games because of the good show he put on," his wife Lucille recalled. "There used to be a saying around town that they'd close the banks to see Norvell umpire."[60] In 1910, he took a job as the projectionist and general manager in Milledgeville's first movie house, the Palace, across the street from the hotel. Three years later, convinced that he could do better than the actors he saw on the screen, he moved to Florida looking for work in the budding film industry there.

Until it was torn down in 1970, the Baldwin Hotel stood at the corner of Wayne and Greene Street, just two blocks from the Cline Mansion at 311 West Greene Street. O'Connor's aunt Katie, who was the mail order clerk in the post office on West Hancock Street, around the corner from the hotel, could have easily passed by every day on her way to work. Since Barty was the more popular of the brothers, she may have wondered that Norvell, the kid people called "Fatty," would be the one to make it big.[61]

O'Connor's celebrity as a cartoonist at GSCW may have brought the town's other, already famous comedian to mind. A brief salute to Oliver Hardy appears in the May 2, 1944, issue of *The Colonnade*, along with O'Connor's cartoon about the campus serving as a winter resort for stray dogs:

The Alumnae Association can profitably point with pride at outstanding GSCW graduates throughout the state. All of us know someone who lived in a Milledgevillian environment at one time, but GMC can claim one celebrated celebrity among its legions of former students. You have seen the face of this man time and time again on the proverbial silver screen, but he's not a glamour boy as so many Jimmies would like to be. Quite the contrary! He makes people laugh. Have you guessed? No, not Lou Costello, Abbot, or Stan Laurel, but Oliver Hardy. If you do not believe it, just ask some of the venerable citizens of historic old Milledgeville. Some of them were his classmates.[62]

In other ways O'Connor's cartoon characters appear to echo memorable images from Laurel and Hardy routines. In one of her cartoons for the "Publications" section of the 1944 *Spectrum*, a long-faced, confused-looking girl comically scratches the hair on the very top of her head in

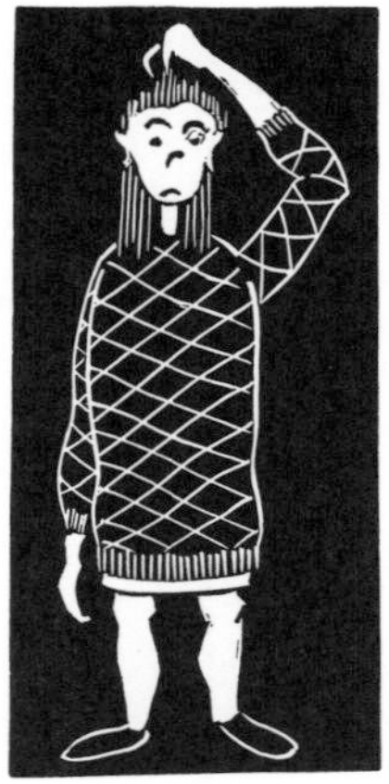

a signature Stan Laurel move. The disapproving frown worn by many of her characters, expressing their irritation at having to endure some ridiculous statement or behavior, is reminiscent of a Hardy "slow burn," a frowning look of disappointment or exasperation with his partner's antics that he would address to the camera.

Hardy facing the audience in mock irritation solicited viewers to identify with his frustration and have a laugh at his exaggerated, ill-tempered reaction. His fans learned to anticipate these pauses, and reading Hardy's face became as much a part of enjoying the performance as the slapstick. The scowling girls in O'Connor's cartoons have a similar effect, but these expressions can also be viewed as another form of O'Connor's self-mockery. As she once wrote to a friend: "I come from a family where the only emotion respectable to show is irritation. In some this tendency produces hives, in others literature, in me both."[63] The tendency also produced some cartoons.

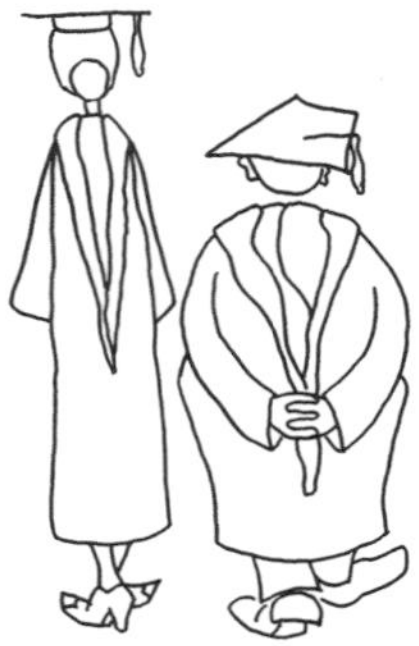

Likewise, her drawing in the 1945 *Spectrum* of a short, rotund figure walking with a tall, thin one, both wearing graduation regalia, could be seen as an impression of Laurel and Hardy inspired by their 1940 film *A Chump at Oxford*, in which both comedians wore mortar boards and scholar's robes. But as Love recalls, these two figures were caricatures of people much closer to home, and no student who saw it "needed a caption to identify the Dean of Women and the Academic Dean."[64] Surely, it couldn't be that the school's administration was in the hands of two bumbling, well-intentioned clowns. (Substitute the mortar boards for two bowler hats.)

It wouldn't be the only time O'Connor's admiration for comic actors showed up in her work. A W. C. Fields bit gets a rerun in one of her

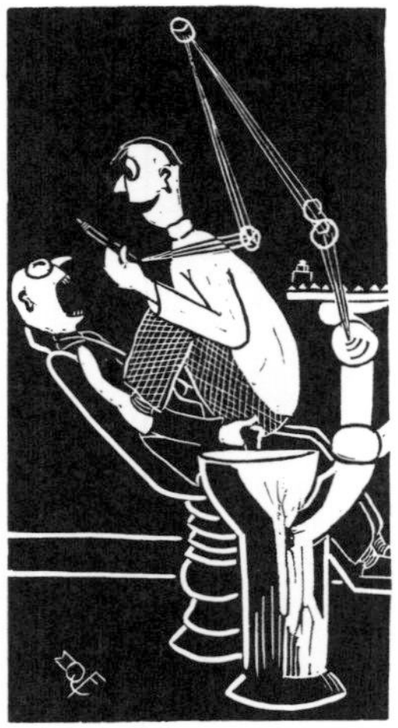

final cartoons for *The Colonnade*, "You don't mind if I get comfortable, do you?" published May 22, 1945. In the 1932 Mack Sennett comedy *The Dentist*, Fields maneuvers himself between the legs of his female patient reclining in the chair while he drills her teeth in one of the film's funniest, and raunchiest, sequences. In a reversal typical of her sense of humor, O'Connor inverts the image in her cartoon which has the dentist climbing into the chair astride the patient's midsection, drill in hand. Writing to Hester in 1963, O'Connor reported, "The other day I postponed my work an hour to look at W. C. Fields in *Never Give a Sucker an Even Break*. This indicates the measure of my respect for Mr. Fields."[65] She followed this with a lengthy assessment of the film and mused, part in fantasy and part in recognition of her affinity with his style, that she "might have written a picture that would be good for him. But it would have been all him."[66]

There has been some speculation that O'Connor and her friend Betty Boyd, as she was known then, were the original models for the stocky girl and her tall companion seen so often in the cartoons. Boyd and O'Connor were both enrolled in the accelerated program and met during their first semester at GSCW, in the summer of 1942. They were studious and serious-minded, and they shared a passion for writing. *The Corinthian* published work by both young women. Boyd was later elected president of the student government. "They were so close," recalls their friend Jane Parks Willingham. "They had a kindred spirit. Yet Betty was not awkward like Flannery. She was a very polished person, and much more into things on campus."[67] Boyd was clearly one of O'Connor's best friends during their college days, and their closeness led Betty's roommate, Mary Boyd (no relation), to constantly remark on O'Connor's apparent lack of interest in men.[68] When Betty Boyd married in 1949, O'Connor wrote to her, "This should reassure Mary Boyd."[69]

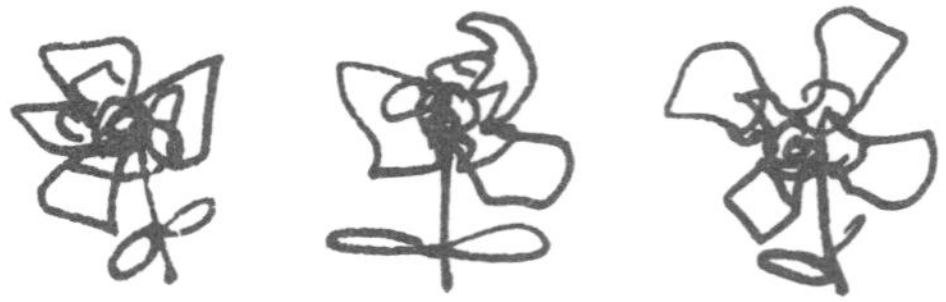

RIGHT: In response to Betty Boyd's announcement of her engagement to James Love in 1949, O'Connor wrote to offer her blessings and an "abundance of peace." She inserted this drawing between the lines of her text, as if it were part of the sentence. "The following are violets," she wrote, followed by her sketch, "or at least I would have you think of them as such. Marriages are always a shock to me." [Letter to Betty Boyd, November 11, 1949, *Habit of Being*, 19.]

and '40s, his work was frequently anthologized. Nash was best known for his light verse about animals involving puns, whimsical rhymes, and creative spellings. His work was clever, deceptively childlike, and he often made irreverent observations, a style and a kind of wit Hines invites readers to relate to O'Connor's lines in her book "Mistaken Identity":

> Now Herman was a happy duck for he enjoyed life
> Until we thought it would be nice if he could have a wife
> And so, we bought him three of them, they were all perfect ladies —
> But Herman took one look and honked, "You Gals can go to Hades!"
> And then one day I saw the light — the truth down to a dreg —
> For the point of the story came to me when Herman laid an egg.[70]

In Nash's poem "The Ostrich," he observes: "It has such long and lofty legs, / I'm glad it sits to lay its eggs." Gooch notes another kinship with Nash in that both writers have a taste for lampooning the works of literary giants. In one of her early satires, "Recollections of My Future Childhood," composed while she was a student at Peabody, O'Connor mimics Proust's *Remembrance of Things Past*. A madeleine cookie is Proust's trigger releasing childhood memories; O'Connor's delectation is a sardine. Gooch compares this to work Nash was doing in the 1930s, like his spoof of James Joyce in "Portrait of an Artist as a Prematurely Old Man."[71]

Another artist known for his work in *The New Yorker* may have had the greater influence on O'Connor's visual style, as well as her early ambition to combine a career in cartooning and writing. That was James Thurber. The similarity was recognized early on by people at GSCW. *The Colonnade*'s features editor, Bee McCormack, was one of them. She claimed, "I thought then she might become the new James Thurber."[72]

Thurber was a household name when O'Connor was growing up, and his drawings and stories inspired Broadway plays, films, and television sitcoms into the 1970s. At the height of his career, his reputation as an American humorist was second only to Mark Twain's.

He was prolific in the 1930s and '40s. Not only was he writing and cartooning for *The New Yorker*, he was publishing a book about every two years. *The Thurber Carnival*, an anthology of his cartoons, stories, and other short pieces, was published in 1945. It became his most popular collection and inspired a 1960 Broadway revue of the same name,

— THURBER AND OTHER INFLUENCES —

The origins of O'Connor's two-girl comedy routine are imminently worth exploring, but there are other influences to consider as well. Calling O'Connor a "female Ogden Nash," Hines summons up another comparison, though more directed to O'Connor's stories about animals, told in rhymes, than related to her cartoon illustrations for them. Nash, whose poems regularly appeared in *The New Yorker*, was both a popular poet and one respected by the literary establishment. Widely known in the 1930s

LEFT: O'Connor (right), editor of the *The Corinthian*, with Mary Jo Brewton, editor of *The Spectrum*, on the steps of Parks Hall, 1945.

directed by Burgess Meredith. Like the book, the stage revue was a compilation of his most popular works, including sketches of his fables, his story "The Night the Bed Fell," and his illustrated parable *The Last Flower* (1939). In the opening act, "World Dance," the dancers paused to deliver lines from Thurber's cocktail cartoons whenever there was a break in the music. His most famous short story, "The Secret Life of Walter Mitty," was published in *The New Yorker* in 1939 and appeared in his 1942 book *My Life and Welcome to It*. In 1947, the story was made into a film starring Danny Kaye. The Technicolor version may have faded a bit with time, but Thurber's original remains a classic of American literature. His "Secret Life" title continues to inspire imitators.

Thurber's line drawings were minimalist and deceptively simple. He used as few strokes as necessary to give his creations substance, concentrating on the essence of a situation or an impression rather than its material details. He was spare in creating facial expressions and allowed the attitude and positioning of bodies, often themselves little more than an outline, to communicate with unencumbered clarity. In these and other ways, O'Connor's cartoons share a kinship with his.

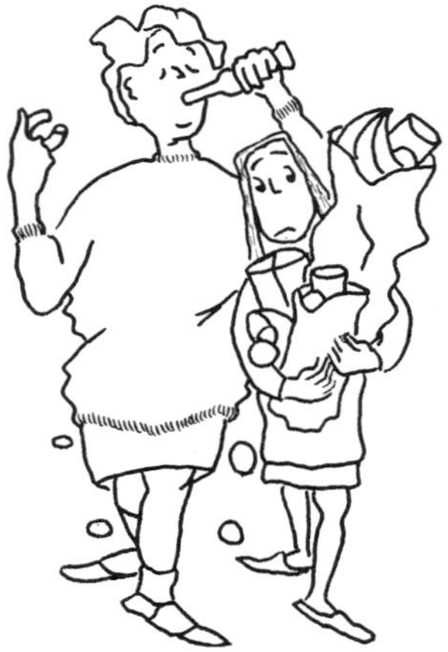

The faces she constructed for her cartoon characters read like a Thurber study. Like his, O'Connor's faces were a simple circle or oval. Most frequently, she used only dots for the eyes. The shape and position of the eyebrows, made of single-line slashes or arches, were the primary cues for attitude and emotion. The triangular noses jutting out from the faces at varying lengths — sometimes a beak, sometimes elongated like a carrot — are also comparable. For both cartoonists, the one-line stroke that was used for the mouth became a semi-circle or wedge, cutting into the face when a character spoke, like a section extracted from a pie. O'Connor's characters in conversation also duplicate a mainstay of Thurber's style, with one character speaking while a companion looks on with an irritated, dissatisfied, or indifferent expression. This monologue-reaction scenario was a basic setup for both of them.

Her images for the 1945 *Spectrum* bear the most astonishing resemblance to Thurber. The spare, more nebulous drawings she made for the yearbook are an obvious imitation of his style. The influence of his draftsmanship is easy to trace there, with her simple ensemble compositions, her thickly drawn bodies and clothes barely an outline, and the essential, expressive faces composed of a few interchangeable elements. Like Thurber, O'Connor's minimalist impressions enabled her to clearly communicate thoughts and emotions and to embody human situations, unencumbered by any unnecessary business in the drawing.

In his introduction to O'Connor's collection of stories *Everything That Rises Must Converge*, Robert Fitzgerald writes that for *The Spectrum* "she tried a rounder kind of comic drawing, not so good," preferring the style of her linocuts to the yearbook's more Thurber-like figures.[73] "In her linoleum cuts the line was always strong and decisive with an energy and angularity that recall the pen drawings of George Price," he wrote.[74] The problem is that Price's drawings, typically identified by his fine, fluid lines and elegant use of detail, are more of a refinement on Thurber's work for *The New Yorker* and don't correspond to Fitzgerald's description. It seems more likely that Fitzgerald had in mind someone like John Held, Jr.

Held was also among the most recognized cartoonists and illustrators of the 1920s and '30s, and, as chance would have it, when O'Connor was beginning her work as a student cartoonist in the fall of 1940, Held was beginning a year as Artist in Residence at the University of Georgia in Athens, about seventy miles north of Milledgeville. When his appointment was announced in the September 23, 1940, issue of *Time*, the "slightly shopworn" artist, or so he was labeled, was still a big enough deal to impress the Carnegie Foundation, which funded his residency.[75]

During his heyday, Held was a syndicated cartoonist, as well as a regular contributor to *The New Yorker*, *Vanity Fair*, *Life*, *College Humor*, and *Judge*, among others, and his style inspired many imitators, including the drawings of a young William Faulkner in Oxford, Mississippi. Held's work provided a template for Faulkner's willowy, long-limbed drawings of flappers and sheiks published around 1920 in the University of Mississippi yearbook, *Ole Miss*, and the student magazine, *The Scream*.[76] Held's caricatures of the "flaming youth" of Jazz Age America, typified by his Joe College and Betty Coed cartoons, together with the more quirky, mischief-loving humor of his woodcuts and linocuts, are elements of his work that would have appealed to O'Connor's ironic sense of humor and her innate talent for mimicry and social satire. He would have made a natural model for her own cartoons about what the college kids were up to, or what the ones at GSCW were up to. Occasionally there is a more direct correspondence between a Held cartoon and one of O'Connor's, such as with her joke about the girl in glasses in "Oh, well, I can always be a Ph.D." In Held's drawing

"There was a dark form at the other end of the bench," from the '20s, it's a short, rather plain-looking young man in large round glasses who sits despondent at the opposite end of the bench from his date, who is turning away, rejecting him.[77]

If Held's presence at a neighboring Georgia university had gone unnoticed by O'Connor and those around her, his wide popularity during her childhood would have made his work accessible and memorable. O'Connor's cartoons at GSCW, like Faulkner's at Ole Miss, appear to reflect some of the features of Held's visual style. In O'Connor's case, the decisive lines and curved angularity of her figures, the occasional bold stripes and polka dot patterns in the clothes, the gangling arms and legs jutting about in rhythmical chaos on a dance floor or figures with limbs flung about in disarray like unstrung marionettes — all bear testimony to Held's influence.

Fitzgerald might not have been a fan of Thurber, but O'Connor's cartoons in Thurber's "rounder" style were such a hit with the students at GSCW that before O'Connor left for graduate school at Iowa, she painted some of her cartoons from the 1945 *Spectrum* on the walls of the student center in the basement of Parks Hall, where the office for student publications was located. One of her cartoon murals can be seen in a 1948 issue of *The Alumnae Journal*. In the background of a photo of Carol Jean Cason, the alumnae secretary for that year, the lower half of one of O'Connor's murals is visible.[78] It's a reproduction of the cartoon "They Guide Us on Our Way," the Laurel and Hardy figures in graduation robes. One of O'Connor's teachers, Helen Greene, wrote that "Mary Flannery... never did discuss the *New Yorker* with me; but James Thurber was one of its shining lights then, and her own ability at drawing his very same kind of people and animals provided delightful decoration for our student publications."[79] Green recalls that these "Thurber-esque types" remained on the walls in Parks for many years.[80]

Thurber, well-known for his drawings of basset hounds, was a bit like O'Connor in drawing her pet chickens; he drew the same one over and over again. Thurber's dogs were a favorite subject of his and of his fans, and a favorite theme running through his work. Dorothy Parker, in her 1943 introduction to *Thurber's Men Women and Dogs*, writes, "My heart used to grow soft at the sight of his dogs; now it turns completely liquid."[81] O'Connor, perhaps mocking the popularity of Thurber's dogs, comes up with a few long-eared hounds of her own. She makes fun of the stray dogs wandering the campus and describes the odd behavior of these "students" in "Going to the Dogs," published in the Fall 1942 *Corinthian*. The sophistication sometimes taken on by Thurber's dogs

was for her narrator not entirely admirable. "The audacity of the stray hound who lopes leisurely into a Fine Arts class can hardly be coped with in any diplomatic manner," her narrator huffed.[82]

Her cartoon of a pack of these sophisticated hounds in the May 2, 1944, issue of *The Colonnade* has them complaining about the accommodations: "The whole family's been wintering here at GSCW — you have to take what you can get these days." An attitude of ironic superiority is taken up by an almost identical-looking pack of Thurber dogs in a cartoon reprinted in the 1966 collection, *Thurber and Company*. Five dogs lounging on a hillside observe a woman walk by, followed by a man with a glum face and a small, angry-looking girl. One of Thurber's dogs remarks, "There go the most intelligent of all animals."[83]

O'Connor's cartoons show a flair for the surreal from time to time. Like Thurber with his talking dogs, often more human than his humans, she also occasionally incorporates animals that nudge the cartoon into an altered reality — in one a giant turkey on a leash, in another a talking

ABOVE: One of O'Connor's murals reproducing a cartoon from the 1945 *Spectrum* is visible in the background of this 1948 photo of the alumnae secretary, Carol Jean Cason, seated at a booth in the student center. O'Connor's cartoons remained on the walls in Parks Hall for many years.

eagle with an enormous bent beak. In Thurber's cartoons, women recline in the moon like a cradle, their faces, gargantuan, melt into the backs of houses, and mysterious figures heave into the picture from above enveloped in darkness and thunder. O'Connor's cartoon girls read books standing on their heads, fall into unexplained holes in the ground and pop out of them again in another location like gophers, they can leap over other students like giant frogs, and their eyes can snake out of their heads and down the street in the opposite direction to ogle boys passing by on the sidewalk.

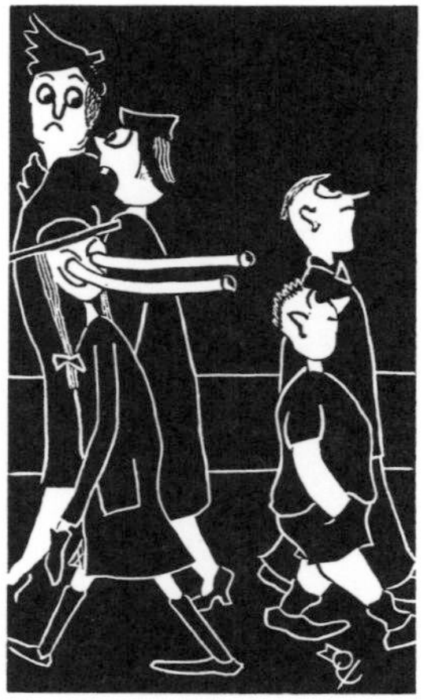

"He [Thurber] pooh-poohs the tendency of art critics to breathe his name with that of Matisse and Picasso," claims a 1943 *Time* magazine review of *Thurber's Men, Women, and Dogs*. "But his drawings have long been taken seriously by advanced students of fantasy, and one sketch of a lady's alcoholic visions was hung (under the heading of Miracles and Anomalies) at the outstanding Fantastic Art-Dada-Surrealism show at Manhattan's Museum of Modern Art in 1936."[84] Thurber may not have been entirely willing to see his cartoons as fit comparisons to Matisse and Picasso, but his impressionistic style and experiments with surrealism indicate otherwise.

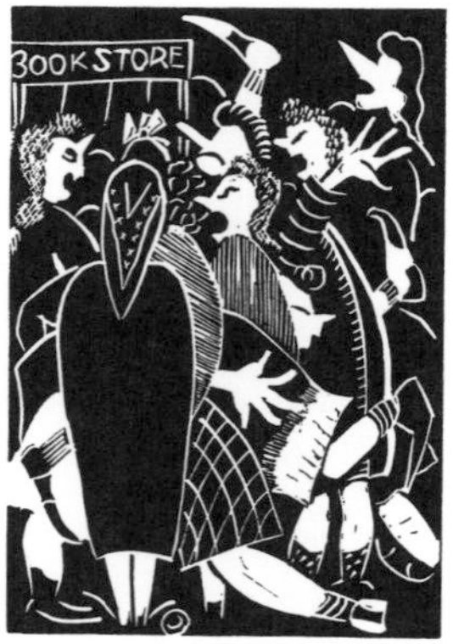
BOOKSTORE

O'Connor, likewise, was an art student interested in painting and may have been inspired by modernist works she studied. The style of her 1943 cartoon for *The Colonnade* "Business as Usual," with it's fragmented images, floating heads, and severed limbs, is reminiscent of Picasso's *Guernica* (1937). The cartoon is a wartime satire mocking the impact of rationing on college life and the patriotic language of an article adjacent to the cartoon, which challenged GSCW's students to prove "our men in service shall not do all of the fighting."[85] The severe angularity and the duplicated, refracted shapes seen in other cartoons, like "I wonder if there could be anything to that business about studying at the first of the quarter?" in the December 14, 1943, *Colonnade* and "This can never be done in ten minutes" from the January 18, 1944, issue, also show a Cubist-inspired sensibility. The curved limbs of dancing figures in an earlier cartoon from *The Peabody Palladium*, "These Two Express the Universal Feeling of Heart-Brokenness Over School Closing," are reminiscent of figures in Matisse's *Dance* (1910). In the spring of 1945, a small article in *The Colonnade* noted the recognition O'Connor was gaining, not as a cartoonist but as a painter. "O'Connor, Sperry, Anderson Honored" announced that a painting of hers, titled *Winter*, had been selected for a statewide exhibit that would tour Georgia that year.[86] Her involvement with painting would turn out to be more than a passing interest.

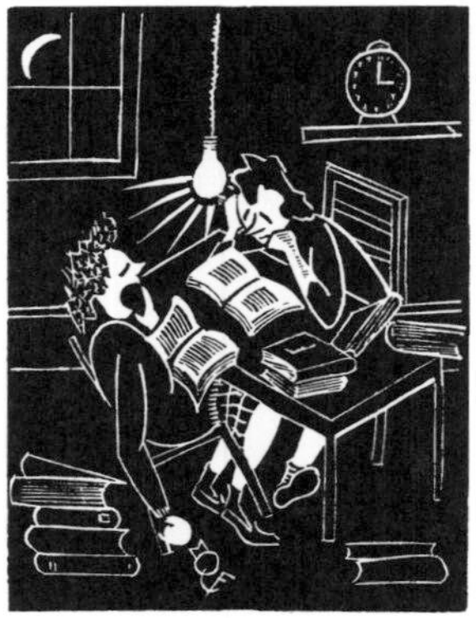

While a student at GSCW, O'Connor submitted numerous cartoons to *The New Yorker* but was not successful in placing her work there. In a 1963 letter to a New York friend, Janet McKane, O'Connor wrote: "I like cartoons. I used to try to do them myself, sent a batch every week to the *New Yorker*, all rejected of course. I just couldn't draw very well. I like the ones that are drawn well better than the situations."[87] The problem may not have been the quality of her cartoons, but the popularity of Thurber. He had many imitators, and *The New Yorker* must have been flooded with submissions from Thurber wannabes. Eudora Welty, another Southern writer and O'Connor's contemporary, was one of them. In 1933, just out of college and looking for work in New York City, Welty wrote to the magazine asking for a job: "How I would like to work for you! A little paragraph each morning — a little paragraph each night, if you can't hire me from daylight to dark, although I would work like a slave. I can also draw like Mr. Thurber, in case he goes off the deep end."[88]

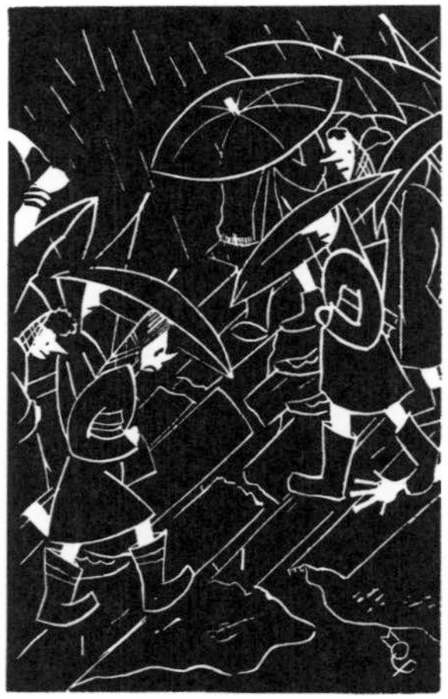

Coincidental or a memory of Thurber, it's hard to say, but writing years later about the nature of violence in her fiction, O'Connor summons one more description of him, this one biographical. She explained, "to the hard of hearing you shout, and for the almost-blind you draw large and startling figures."[89] Thurber lost an eye in a childhood accident and suffered from vision problems his whole life. After undergoing surgeries for cataracts and trachoma in the early 1940s, Thurber slowly began to go blind, but his work didn't stop. There were, however, adjustments made for his declining vision. He would draw his cartoons on very large sheets of white paper with a thick black crayon, or, to improve the contrast, he would draw in white on large sheets of black paper. The cartoons were then reduced, and, if drawn on the black background, the image color was reversed prior to publication. Thurber, almost blind, drew large and startling figures for as long as his sight held out.

— WHAT JESSIE KNEW —

O'Connor was GSCW's own personal Thurber in the years she spent there, but it wasn't all Thurber all the time. She was using her cartoons as an opportunity to portray herself and other people at GSCW; she was also including familiar scenes from campus and college life, recognizable enough to lend her work a documentary flair. Her cartoons certainly hold up as individual works separate from their historical context, but an appreciation for what Peabody and GSCW students would have recognized in them aids in understanding the jokes that O'Connor intended them to laugh at.

In almost every issue of the student newspaper where one of O'Connor's cartoons is found, there is at least one editorial or news item that directly corresponds to her cartoon, showing that O'Connor took campus events as her most frequent subjects. This is a trend that began with her work in high school for *The Peabody Palladium* and continued in *The Colonnade*.

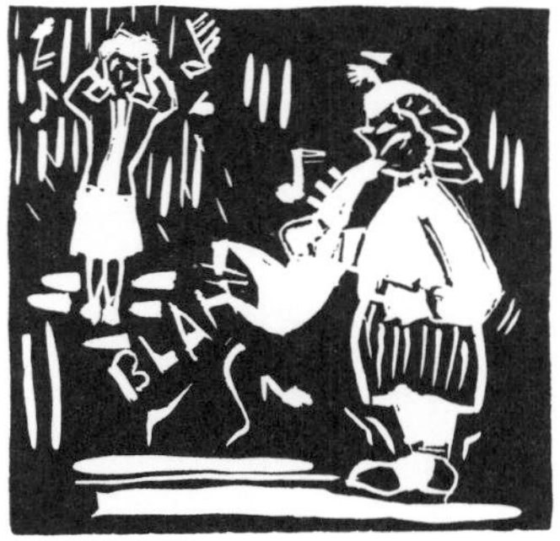
BLAH

Her first cartoon for the *Palladium*, "One Result of the New Peabody Orchestra," published October 28, 1940, responds to an announcement on the front page: "Orchestra and Music Club Are Organized."[90] "The orchestra and the 'Music Lover's Club' are two new organizations that have been started by the music minded people in Peabody," the article reports. According to the

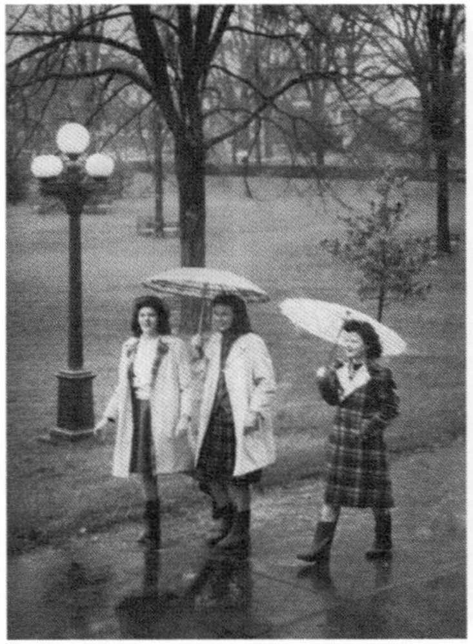

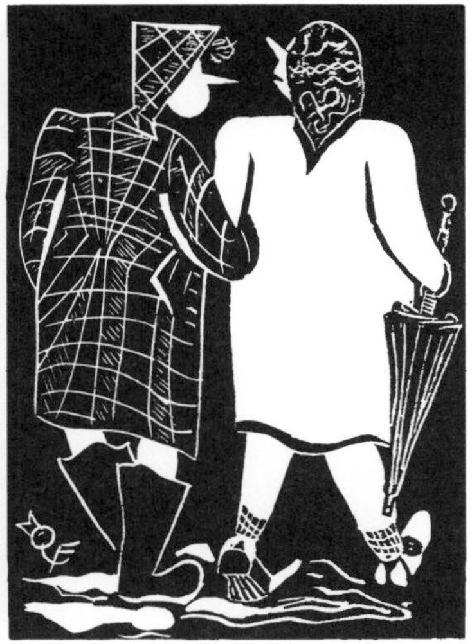

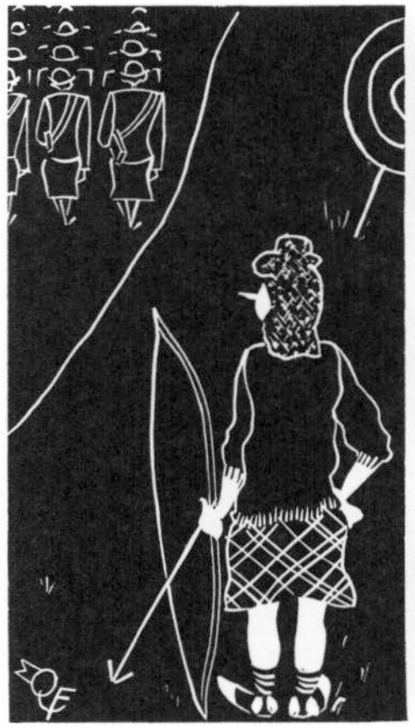

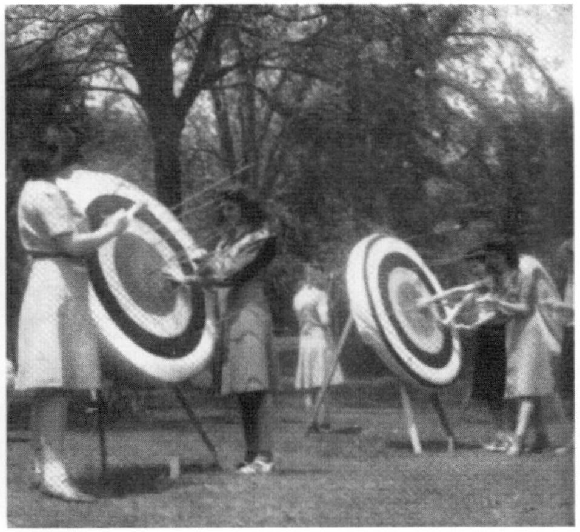

TOP ROW: The many cartoons of students in raingear were not strictly a product of O'Connor's imagination. It seemed to rain a lot in Milledgeville, and girls carrying umbrellas, tromping to class in galoshes and raincoats, would have been a familiar part of the GSCW experience, as documented in this campus photo from *The Spectrum* and one of O'Connor's cartoons, both from 1942.

MIDDLE ROW: O'Connor's cartoons of students taking aim at the invading WAVES with bows and arrows reflect another common campus scene, archery practice. The sport was a popular school activity, as this photo from the 1943 *Spectrum* shows. O'Connor develops her combat theme by suggesting WAVES as alternate targets in this cartoon made the same year.

cartoon, it appears that the music-minded are not always the music-talented, and at least one girl may be planning to keep her distance from this school activity. The school's music programs were the subject of at least one other cartoon, "Music Appreciation Hath Charms," which has a girl snoozing in her chair with her legs stretched out and her arm hanging to the side as bars of music float in her direction. The *Palladium* regularly reported on the school's Music Appreciation Hour held one morning each week, naming the class that hosted, who participated, and what records were played. O'Connor later wrote of herself that she not only had a "tin leg," but also a "tin ear."[91] She was sent to piano lessons and tried her hand at the accordion and the bass violin, but music was never quite her thing. The only time Regina ever recalled spanking her daughter was to make her wear hose to her first piano recital.[92]

Her December 18, 1940, cartoon for the *Palladium*, "'Twas the Night Before Press Time," shows a student hammering away at a typewriter with the pages dropping from the back of the machine to the floor. Two front-page articles about the *Palladium* explain the occasion. "Palladium Joins Press Association" reports that with the current issue the paper had become a member of the Georgia Scholastic Press Association for the first time and detailed the benefits of this achievement. Also on page one, "Journalism Class Edits Palladium" notes the "December issue of *The Peabody Palladium* was published by the Journalism class of the Junior class"[93] as its final project. O'Connor, the paper's art editor and also a junior, gives us a sample of what that was like in her cartoon. Everyone who had been caught up in the whirr of preparing that issue and felt the last-minute punishment of struggling to meet the publication deadline would have appreciated the joke, and the recognition.

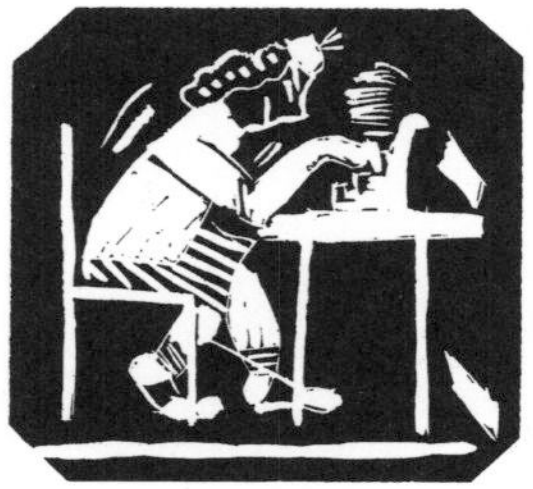

One of her final cartoons for the high school paper, "In Hopes That a Jimmie Soon Will Be There," published December 12, 1941, only a few days after the attack on Pearl Harbor, takes on a different tone. Here she has a girl sitting next to a fireplace with a military-style jacket

RIGHT: "Snooped Scoops" and "Kampus Kapers" are the linocut column headers O'Connor created for use in *The Peabody Palladium* after she became art editor in the fall of 1940. "Snooped Scoops" was a gossip column that usually focused on the dating scene among Peabody girls. "Kampus Kapers" provided a regular review of student activities. The linocut headers first appeared in the *Palladium* in December 1940 and continued to be used through 1941.

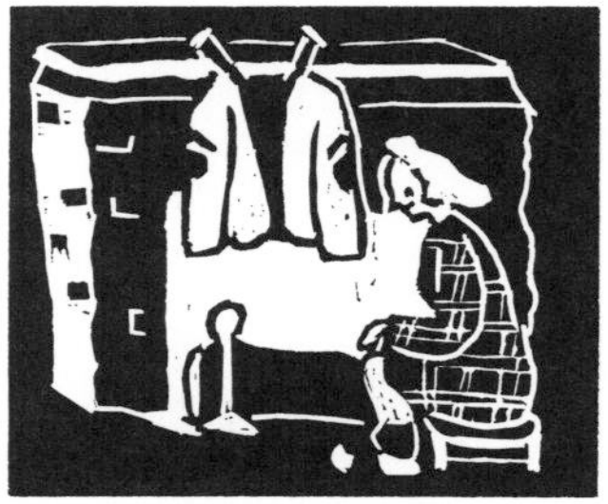

hanging from the mantle as a Christmas stocking. Students at Georgia Military College, a few blocks from Peabody High School and Georgia State College in Milledgeville, were called "Jimmies," a counterpart to the "Jessies" at the women's college. Their nicknames were made by eliding the initials for each school.

Not only were the cadets of GMC the primary source for dates among the Peabody girls, since most of their students were enrolled in GMC's high school division, it was now clear that these young men soon would be called upon to fight overseas. Following the more significant news about the U.S. declaration of war and the upcoming Christmas program dedicated to "Peace," the *Palladium* ran a gossip column that reported, among other juicy bits, who at Peabody was dating whom. In the December 12 issue, "Snooped Scoops" covered these romances with militaristic fervor, reporting on the "latest developments on the Peabody front." Some of the maneuvers were described as follows: "The territory around Regina Sullivan's heart has been occupied by Billy Carr's troops. Little resistance was offered by Regina." "Annie has begun a rearmament program. She's building a wall around Paul Durden for defense against conspirators." [94] And "We have just received a dispatch from Ann Smith stating that her next objective will be George Napier." Once, when a fellow GSCW student praised her creativity in a writing class, O'Connor is reported to have replied, "I'd exchange it for your ability to attract men."[95]

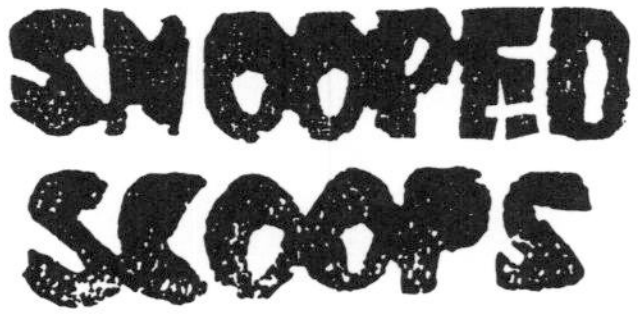
SNOOPED
SCOOPS

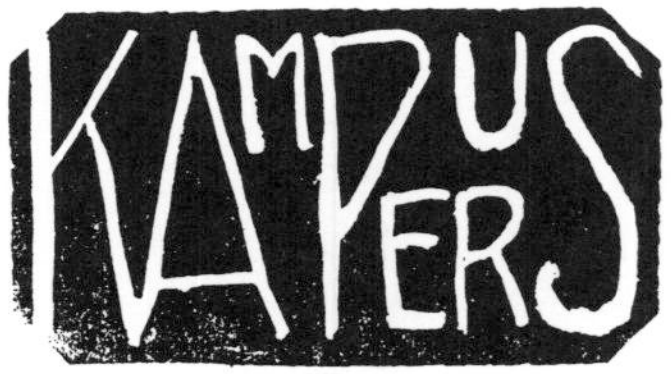
KAMPUS KAPERS

The trend of commenting on school news and events continued with her work in the college newspaper. Her first cartoon for *The Corinthian*, like her first for the *Palladium*, remarks on the negative results of a school activity. "The Immediate Results of Physical Fitness Day" published October 9, 1942, responded to an important campus-wide initiative. An article titled "Keeping Fit: Physical Fitness Program to be Daily Feature at GSCW" highlighted the new program as part of a wartime initiative to

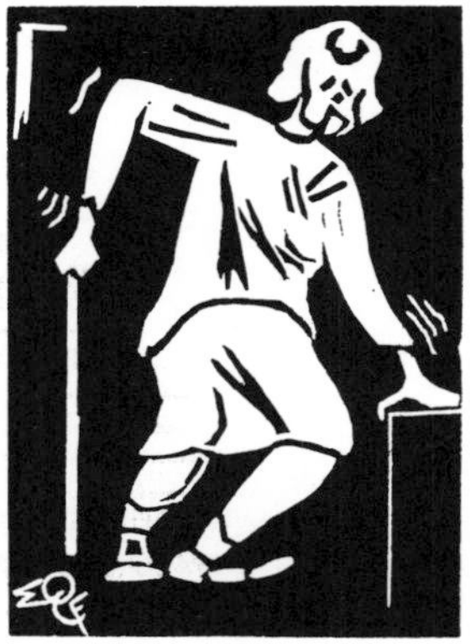

keep "Miss. GSCW" in shape so that "her body will be able to stand up under the multiple strains and tasks of war."[96]

In "The Immediate Results of Physical Fitness Day" a student is hunched over and shakily supporting herself by holding onto the furniture and staggering along with a cane. It borrows its inspiration, in part, from the description provided by Jewell Willie in "Oh, How We Hate To Get Up The Week After Being Fit," published on the same page as the cartoon: "Just as last Saturday was Physical Fitness Day, today is un-Physical Fitness Day. Has there ever been such a week? Sunday, I believe was worse than the other day. We, please don't tell me I am alone in this, were in such a dire state that getting out of bed was torture of inquisitional intensity. Every muscle in our collective anatomies was corroded by every fatigue acid ever invented. We behaved like homing pigeons every time we beheld a pillow — or even a chair."[97] Willie begs someone to please pass the Absorbine Jr. before it's all gone.

O'Connor continued in this vein with *The Colonnade*, taking inspiration from the headlines or passages from stories in the paper, as well as from her own observations and projected scenarios for her cartoon Jessies. She also had her eye on the arts scene on campus and didn't miss the opportunity to satirize the annual theater competition, which involved some pretty outrageous behavior and her good friend Betty Boyd, who had a prominent role in producing the freshman entry. The result is O'Connor's cartoon "Doggone this Golden Slipper Contest. Now we have to wear saddle oxfords" in the November 14, 1942, *Colonnade*.

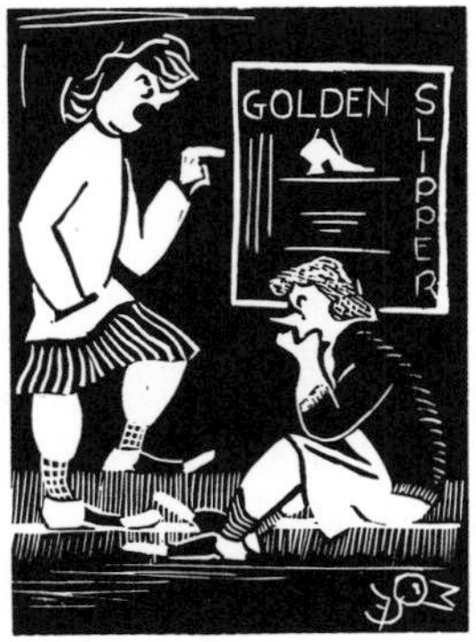
GOLDEN SLIPPER

The Golden Slipper was a drama contest between the freshman and sophomore classes created to help homesick and disoriented newcomers bond with their sister class. A gold-plated ornamental shoe picked up on a New York shopping trip by one of the deans was the trophy that got traded back and forth each year. The tradition at GSCW was that the freshman and junior classes, and the sophomore and senior classes, were considered "sisters."[98] The competition, first held in 1935, was not only a creative and spirited event but an occasion for the upperclassmen to cheer and encourage the underclassmen and form a sisterly bond. The freshman entry, "Blossoms on Bataan," was written by Margaret Meaders, dramatized by Betty Boyd, and directed by Tommie Maxwell.[99]

The opening of the event involved a lot of elaborate taunting and a preliminary skit from each side. That year's skits showed four freshmen "searching through catalogues for a shoe for their opponents to wear instead of the Golden Slipper."[100] The sophomores followed up with a mock funeral for a "bewailing" freshman.

The decorations that the competing sister classes made for the auditorium were equally provocative: "At 8 p.m. the entire student body gathered in Russell Auditorium to witness the gala occasion," *The Colonnade* reported on November 14. "Here, original decorations adorned the respective sides of the competitive classes. Two disconsolate, shoeless sophs, and a gleeful, golden slippered frosh could be seen on the wall of the freshman side, while a negro mammy gazed proudly at her golden slippered foot on the sophomore side."[101]

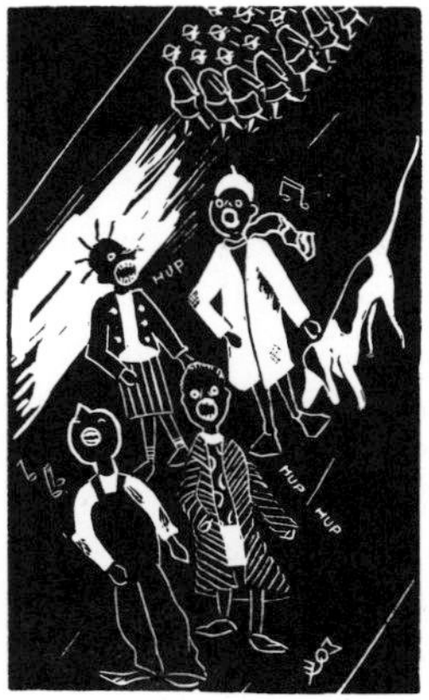

Apparently, some of the girls also attended in blackface, as a column published by the paper the following May recalls: "Do you remember the smeared black faces straining toward the stage at the Golden Slipper Contest?"[102] This impression of students in blackface shows up in one of O'Connor's cartoons the following year, "Two mo' monts we won' be a-doin' it," in the February 1, 1944, issue of *The Colonnade*. This cartoon appears to lampoon the WAVES chanting or singing as they marched, while students in blackface HUP HUP along mimicking the WAVES in the background; graduation for Jessies and the women sailors was coming up in May. The caption from this cartoon was repeated in the 1944 *Spectrum* in a mock diary entry from "The News and Views of Jessie Jones as Recorded in Her Diary," the creative device used to recall all the important events of the past year. The "diary" entry for Sunday, November 28: "...two more weeks (plus three days) we won't be a-doin' this."[103] Jessie was marking time till the end of the fall semester. O'Connor, who prepared a series of cartoons for this volume of *The Spectrum*, depicts GSCW's everygirl Jessie Jones propped up in bed in her pajamas with her hair in rollers musing over what to write in her diary.

On the front page of *The Colonnade* in which O'Connor's Golden Slipper cartoon appeared, the article "Frosh Bow to Mighty Sophs In Annual Slipper Contest" described the event and the freshman loss, and helps to make sense of the joke about the saddle oxfords that appears as the caption for the cartoon. The freshmen had taunted the sophomores with a particularly unappealing shoe that they would select for the losers to wear. When the freshmen lost, the tables were turned, but wearing saddle oxfords was no great hardship. If that were a sign that you were a loser, everyone wore them.

After the Golden Slipper hoopla and the Christmas break, a traveling exhibit from the Museum of Modern Art in New York City became another big attraction. "I don't enjoy looking at these old pictures either, but it doesn't hurt my reputation for people to think I'm a lover of fine arts," her cartoon for the January 16, 1943, *Colonnade*, gives O'Connor's take on how it was received among the students at GSCW. The exhibit and the works it included had been covered in each issue of *The Colonnade* since January 2, 1943.

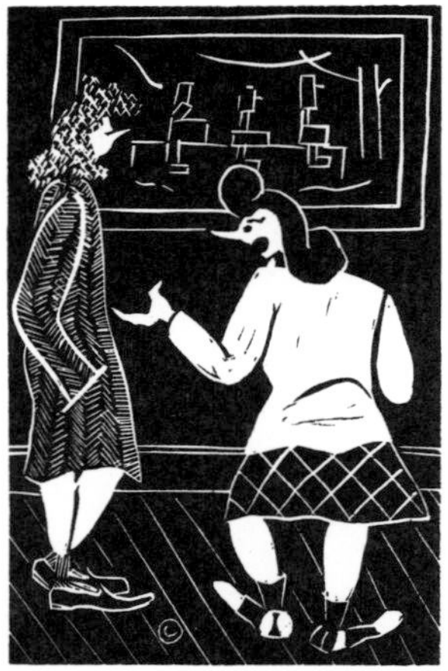

The first of these articles was leading news in the January 2 issue, "CGA and Art Department Will Sponsor Exhibition." Announcing the exhibit opening, it explained that the paintings were reproductions circulated for educational purposes, as an introduction to modern art. In gallery talks offered by the college's art department, students could rely on "Miss Mamie Padgett to fully explain not only the picture itself, but each movement and line the artist has suggested."[104]

"Art Exhibition in Second Week" in the next issue of *The Colonnade* reports: "The appreciation of good art especially today, means a great deal. For a week there has been an exhibition of works of modern artists in the library of GSCW — painted by some of the fine artists, such as Van Gogh, Daumier, Corot, Cézanne, and others. The exhibition has been booked since December."[105] By the second week, 333 students had signed the guest register, about a third of the young women attending GSCW that year. Of the artists featured in the exhibit, Van Gogh was to make a lasting impression on O'Connor; the brush strokes and coloring of her 1953 self-portrait with a pheasant cock imitate his style. During the final week of the art exhibit, scheduled to close on January 18, students were treated to O'Connor's cartoon interpretation of what the "appreciation of good art" at GSCW was really about.

Beyond the occasions for providing comic illustration or a witty counterpoint to one news item or another, she seemed to strive in her cartoons to hold up a mirror to the hothouse environment of a small-town women's college where its residents could enjoy a laugh of recognition. In Hazel Smith's column "Campus Fashion" in *The Colonnade*, smartly dressed girls could expect to have their wardrobes regularly dissected on the verbal runway. "Doing our usual snooping, we find that plaids and checks have become essentials of the college girl's wardrobe," Smith wrote for a 1942 issue. "Helen Clay, a petite brunette, chose a black, yellow, and red plaid skirt. It has two kick pleats in front and two in the back. She combines white silk and a red cardigan with her outfit."[106]

O'Connor's eye was drawn to the fashion parade, too, but not at the high end of the spectrum. She thrived on eroding the idealized version of the all-American college girl and turned a glaring spotlight on the reality of oversized sweaters hiding dumpy figures, sloppy skirts, frumpy hair, and saddle oxfords and loafers sometimes drawn so large they would embarrass the clowns at Barnum's.

Her fellow students, however, saw something of the truth, and themselves, in her cartoons. "She was a genius at depicting us 'Jessies' running around campus, with scarves hanging out of pockets, or messily draped on our heads," says former student Gertrude Ehrlich.[107] In her article for the Fall 1944 *Corinthian*, "Fashions' Perfect Medium," O'Connor moves her satire of college fashion to prose, writing detailed descriptions of the Jessies' wardrobe choices: "Take sweaters for instance. By now they are practically standard. In fact, there are only two rules which govern their being worn — they must be either four sizes too large or three sizes too small — and since only those who weigh over two hundred and fifty pounds feel inclined to wear them three sizes too small, the oversize sweater is the only one to be considered."[108]

O'Connor wasn't the only catty student to take a swipe at the fashion scene. Joyce Moncrief also shows her claws in "You Can Have My Share," published in the same issue of *The Corinthian*. O'Connor's lino cuts illustrating Moncrief's article depict girls with wildly exaggerated features to match their unladylike behavior. Moncrief breaks down one character for her readers named Tallulah, alternately "Tallulah, the one and only," "Her Royal Highness," and "the girl with the hair-do."[109] She "went to New York three summers ago and never got over it" and "can't utter more than two sentences without dragging in the fact that she

orders her garments from Foofnagles, Inc."[110] As Moncrief rounds out the scene, Tallulah, who never wastes her breath on a "limited audience," is bearing down on a group of unsuspecting freshmen with her copy of *Vogue*. In O'Connor's cartoon, Tallulah's big nose and her big rear end are both elevated to match her attitude. In these distorted figures the predecessors of some of O'Connor's female grotesques in her fiction can be seen, like Sarah Ham in "The Comforts of Home" with her "pointed chin, wide apple cheeks and feline empty eyes"[111] or the woman with the red spear-tipped fingers whom Hazel Motes meets in the dining car on the way to Taulkinham in *Wiseblood*.

"Why don't we do this more often?" O'Connor's cartoon in the October 17, 1942, *Colonnade*, was a salute to Parents' Day, an annual event for family visitors with lunch provided on the front lawn of the campus. "Parents' Day Attracts Many Here Today" was a lead story on page one. Adjacent to the cartoon on page four, another piece about the event, "Welcome, Parents and Friends," gave it a sentimental review as the "highlight of the year."[112] This year, due to wartime tire and gas rationing, the administration did away with the part of the event where residence halls competed for the largest percentage of parents to attend. Parents' Day would be discontinued altogether in subsequent years, for the same reasons. Also on the front page of this issue, students read about another indicator of change, one that would affect their college experience till the end of WWII and become the subject of some of O'Connor's best cartoons: The WAVES.

— AT WAR WITH THE WAVES —

"LATE FLASH," on the first page of the October 17 issue of *The Colonnade*, gave a brief rundown of the Navy's intention to use the campus: "The Navy announced that Women's Naval Reserve Enlisted Corps members will be trained at GSCW, sent letter intent for use of campus. No contract yet, but first class starts on January 15th, with 400."[113] The influx of WAVES, or Women Appointed for Voluntary Emergency Ser-

vice, would cause on-going competition for space and resources for the next three years, as well as inspiring some curiosity and envy among the Jessies. Elizabeth Knowles Adams recalls, "Some of us were probably a little jealous because they seemed so glamorous in their uniforms."[114]

From 1943 to 1945, 15,000 WAVES were trained at GSCW; among them were some WACS, SPARS, and Women Marines who were placed there temporarily while they waited for their bases to open.[115] The WAVES took over four of the college's residence halls (Ennis Hall, Mansion Annex, Mayfair Hall, and Sanford) requiring GSCW students to crowd three and four to a room. Even getting to and from classes was difficult for the Jessies, as they had to dodge the formations of WAVES that seemed to be forever marching up and down the campus walkways and through the town; part of their training regimen required WAVES to march sixteen miles every day. "They'd get out every morning at six marching between the dining hall and the library," Jane Sparks Willingham remembered. "It wasn't a happy mix, but it was necessary."[116]

The crowding and competition for resources caused some grumbling among students, but they were also proud that the small sacrifices they were making directly supported the war effort. The military presence on campus was a daily reminder of their participation in a larger world. O'Connor was later to express it in "The Nature and Aim of Fiction" by pointing out that "it's well to remember that the fiction writer always writes about the whole world, no matter how limited his particular scene." She added, "For him, the bomb that was dropped on Hiroshima affects life on the Oconee River, and there's nothing he can do about it."[117] The WAVES invasion at GSCW gave "home front" a whole new meaning.

In February 1943, the arrival of the first WAVES was the lead story for *The Colonnade*. A lengthy article, "GSCW Welcomes the WAVES," was accompanied by photos of WAVES on campus and marching in formation in front of the college president's house. *The Spectrum* for that year devoted several pages of photographs to the WAVE presence on campus, including snapshots of them as they went about their daily routine. The WAVES remained a huge presence on the campus and in the school publications during the years they trained there. Alongside those photos and stories are O'Connor's cartoons satirizing the response to the Navy presence among the college students.

In her WAVES cartoons, O'Connor has students asking to try on the WAVES's hats and stumbling over Navy jargon, exercising like maniacs to achieve that ideal military physique, climbing trees to avoid being trampled by WAVES marching by in formation, and climbing onto rooftops because the Navy has left them with a shortage of classrooms, as well as

a shortage of dorm rooms. While there is always some news item about the WAVES in the student paper during these years, O'Connor's cartoons about them become increasingly detached from those reports, taking on a story line of their own; they satirized an experience that every student shared and needed no additional background to explain. Margaret Uhler's most vivid memory of O'Connor during her time at GSCW was that "we all scanned the *Colonnade* for her delightful cartoons before we read anything else."[118] Students didn't always need to read the paper to know what the cartoons were about. That was especially true of her cartoons about the WAVES.

O'Connor's WAVES cartoons gave another impression of the war on the home front as they took on the dimensions of mock combat between the invading Navy forces and college students defending their native turf. One cartoon girl stares into the distance at a group of WAVES marching in formation and considers using them for targets during archery practice. In another, a student portrayed as a little girl with a ribbon in her hair, looking like one of Thurber's cartoon children, chases a group of WAVES up a tree with her bow and arrow. Following the combat theme, students' curiosity about the WAVES turned to questions about whether they carried gunpowder in their handbags. As the series progressed, O'Connor began to portray the women in uniform as grownups, the students as children, turning it into a comedy about girls resisting the strictures and conformity demanded in an adult world. The cartoon Jessies' efforts at retaliation descended into a series of juvenile pranks. Surveying a collection of uniforms hanging up on hooks, two students wonder if they can still make the Dean's List if they mix up all the hats. In another cartoon, a Jessie runs behind a formation of WAVES dragging her umbrella across the backs of their legs like the slats in a picket fence. Her final WAVES cartoon for the 1945 *Spectrum*, "Our Naval Escort," depicts one of the WAVES as an annoyed adult with her arms folded across her chest bending forward to face a GSCW student drawn as a little girl who has to reach up to pat her Naval escort on the shoulder.

In one of her cartoons about WAVES, a group of girls stare and point at a pair of sailors

TOP ROW: "Seamen and seniors enjoying an informal moment in late afternoon," a photo from the 1943 *Spectrum*, provides an immaculately staged scene of college students and WAVES enjoying conversation in one of the school's lounges, when in reality the two rarely mixed. O'Connor's cartoon in the 1944 *Spectrum* of students gathered in a similar sitting room tells a different story, of little conversation, wholesale boredom, and girls whose manner and personal appearance are far from photo-ready.

MIDDLE ROW: After the Navy school for WAVES opened at GSCW in early 1943, WAVES marching in formation crowded campus walkways, making it difficult for students to get to and from class. This 1944 photo captures what would have been a daily scene at the college during WWII. O'Connor's cartoon "Traffic" from 1943 shows how one student avoids the onslaught.

in white uniforms walking by. One comments, "Those are the kind of WAVES I like." If a women's college was going to be invaded by the Navy, why couldn't the sailors have been men? This particular wartime shortage prompted students to give the school another name, "Georgia State College of Wallflowers."[119] Men were is short supply, and the influx of women from the Navy made competition for that particular resource even more severe, but the size and importance of the training facility at GSCW was enough to attract one man in particular and gain the college coast-to-coast publicity. An article in the May 15, 1943, *Colonnade*, "Bob Hope Entertains Navy Tonight; Students Invited to Attend Program," announced that Hope's broadcast from Russell Auditorium, scheduled for Tuesday, May 18, 1943, would be "the first time that a coast-to-coast broadcast has ever originated in Milledgeville, and as the Bob Hope Program is one of the most popular on the air, millions of listeners will be tuned in."[120]

An interview with Hope appeared in the next issue of *The Colonnade*, on May 22. Setting Hope up for a joke about the high-density female population of Milledgeville, the interviewer asked if the "Georgia peaches" he encountered on his visit were "all they are supposed to be." Hope fired back, "Fuzzy as ever." How could GSCW's celebrated local cartoonist miss the opportunity to do a

caricature of Hope? Rumor has it she didn't. Hope was known as "old ski nose" and later traded jokes on television with Jimmy Durante about the size of their famous noses. Funny noses were a weakness for O'Connor; they were her favorite cartoon exaggeration. When she was a girl, she had even composed a booklet of words and drawings dedicated just to noses called "Ladies and Gents, Meet the Three Mister Noseys," with drawings titled "Mr. Long Nose," "Mr. Sharp Nose," and "Mr. Snut Nose."[121] Supposedly, when Hope saw O'Connor's cartoon of him he blurted that "looks like hell."

The Navy continued to train women at GSCW till the spring term of 1945, when the last class of WAVES graduated, and so did O'Connor. It was the end of an era for her and for the college. In the fall of 1944, she was tapped for the school's prestigious Phoenix Society, whose members were selected by the Phi Beta Kappa faculty at the college. In the October 24, 1944, *Colonnade*, she was noted as one of only twelve seniors at GSCW to be selected for Who's Who in American Colleges and Universities. The 1945 *Spectrum*, populated with her cartoons, gave her this parting tribute: "Mary Flannery O'Connor's cartoons have given laughs to all."[122]

After leaving GSCW, O'Connor continued her study of the visual arts during her first year of graduate study at the University of Iowa, and took classes in drawing and advertising, although her primary interest soon shifted to writing fiction.[123] Her first year there, she continued to try to sell her cartoons, submitting them to trade journals and hoping, perhaps, the competition for placement would be less intense than at *The New Yorker*.[124] The rejections she continued to receive might have been one reason she felt discouraged about a future in journalism. O'Connor may have stopped submitting her cartoons to magazines, but the skills and the creative habits she developed during her years as a cartoonist continued to serve her well as a fiction writer.

ABOVE: O'Connor (back row, center) and other students selected for Who's Who in American Colleges and Universities pose for a 1945 yearbook photo on the campus lawn. The photo also captures some of the ever-present baggy sweaters, plaid skirts, loafers, and striped socks that she depicts in her cartoons.

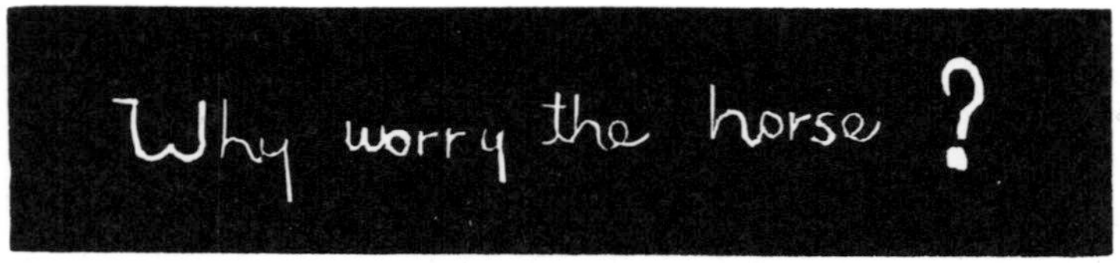
Why worry the horse ?

— DRAWING WITH WORDS —

In a 1955 letter to Ben Griffith, an English professor at Mercer University and a perceptive early critic of her fiction, O'Connor reduced her assessment of good writing to a simple truth: "You have got to learn to paint with words."[125] After she returned to Milledgeville to stay and was living with her mother at Andalusia, she took up painting, again, in a more serious way. She had been a successful painter in college, too, but her cartoons were so much in the foreground that little is known about the other visual art she produced then.

Though there are definitely ways in which her fiction is painterly, she could just as well have told Griffith, "You have got to learn to draw cartoons with words," because a good bit of the time, that was what she was doing.

The creative process she followed in cartooning transferred well to her work in fiction. She knew how to draw a character that could make people laugh and how to use the suggestions made by images to get readers to see what was funny without having to spell it out. She had developed a repertoire of jokes, visual gags, and humorous character types and situations that could come into play when she was developing a story, to help get the ball rolling. Sometimes as she composed, she would laugh out loud over some description, line of dialogue, or bit of business she had just written for one of her characters, as she must have often laughed at her own cartoons before she'd had a chance to share them.

The urge for cartooning can be seen in the superficial sketches she created for some characters in her fiction, pegging them with one or two quirky physical features and allowing them to remain otherwise flat and peripheral. In her story "Revelation," O'Connor puts a few of these in the doctor's waiting room, like the "woman with the snuff-stained lips."[126] On the bus in "Everything That Rises Must Converge" there's the "thin woman with protruding teeth and long yellow hair"[127] and "the woman with the red and white canvas sandals."[128]

ABOVE: *The Corinthian* (Winter 1943): 15. O'Connor provided a custom header for her essay in this issue, "Why worry the horse?" In response to the problems of gasoline rationing and parts shortages during World War II, she facetiously contemplates a return to literal horsepower as a mode of transportation and imagines the horse struggling to adapt. "Signs along the highway, which are to us mere trivialities, to him would be novel and interesting," O'Connor explains. "When informed for the first time that his friends may be avoiding him because he has failed to use the right dandruff preparation, the horse is apt to become distressed beyond conceivable measure."

These simple, vivid impressions are reminiscent of the figures in her cartoons and the attention that she gave to certain features of an otherwise slight composition — a particularly loud pattern in a plaid skirt, a row of wildly grinning teeth, or the texture and shape of some out-of-control amoeba-like hairdo. The minimalist faces described in her fiction also sometimes recall the faces in her cartoons, in their small, seed-like or ice-pick eyes, or in their exaggerated proportions, such as Mr. Shiftlet's head in "The Life You Save May Be Your Own," whose "face descended in forehead for more than half its length" like O'Connor's girl with a gavel in the 1944 *Spectrum*.

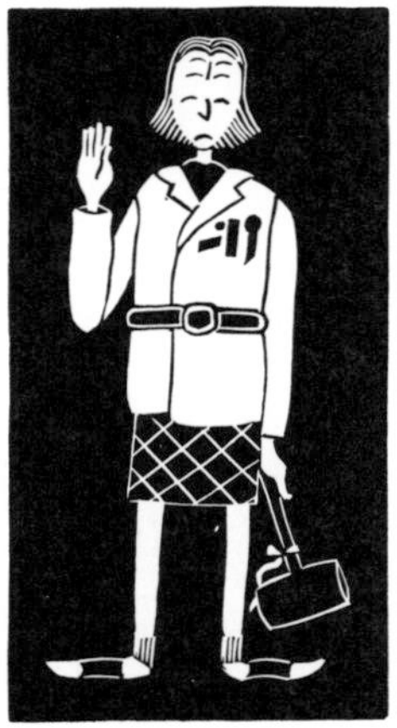

Mr. Shiftlet, appropriately enough, also sleeps with his feet sticking out the window of Lucy Nell Crater's broken-down 1928 Ford, a cartoon-like image that would be perfectly at home in *Li'l Abner* or *Snuffy Smith*, but is also a repeating image in O'Connor's cartoons. She has feet sticking up in the air, sticking out at odd angles, feet of exaggerated proportions propped up on desks and chairs and flexing their toes across the top of a page in an illustrated header for "Effervescence," her satire on the raptures of springtime in the Spring 1943 *Corinthian*. Perhaps her fascination with them had something to do with the corrective shoes she had to wear as a child. A thinly disguised version of herself in a childhood story has a character named "Mary Flemming" in a pair of "Tarso-Supernator-ProperBuilt" orthopedic shoes.[129] The joke goes back at least that far.

She had a habit of working over the same gags again and again, like a relative telling the same stories at every family reunion. And it's not just the fancy footwork. There are jokes about school teachers and trying to avoid their influence. Jokes about pretty girls she makes look ugly and ugly ones that she makes funny, about girls angling for a man and the ones no man would take. And there are jokes that involve inversions and distortions so extreme the world seems to have gone completely wonky, like someone took a bite out of the wrong side of the mushroom. These themes found in her cartoons are woven through her fiction as well.

There were certain personalities and situations that she just thought were funny, and she kept going back to them. The combative, scrappy girls seen in cartoons like "Counter-Attack," from the April 18, 1944, *Colonnade*, and "Madam Chairman, the committee has reached a decision," from the previous issue, are a particular favorite. They return in characters like the child in "A Temple of the Holy Ghost," who is constantly churning up some mischief she can work against her cousins. Sally Virginia in "A Circle in the Fire" is another, strapping on her toy pistols and threatening to beat up the three marauding boys on her mother's farm. Mary Fortune Pitts, a girl of nine in "A View of the Woods," warns her grandfather to take off his glasses before they start fighting. Mary Grace's assault on Mrs. Turpin in "Revelation" is so violent that the girl has to be wrestled to the ground and subdued with an injection. "Ladies don't beat the daylight out of people," Sally Virginia's mother tells her. Studies in good behavior were far from O'Connor's field of interest. As a girl she was known to resist ladylike behavior herself, when she could get away with it. Childhood friend Loretta Feuger Hoynes recalled, "If you wanted her to be a good girl, she was nothing."[130]

The scowling expressions worn by many of O'Connor's cartoon girls are recognizable in the child in "A Temple of the Holy Ghost" with her "frigid frown,"[131] in Sally Virginia's "frowning squint" and "furious outraged look,"[132] in Mary Fortune Pitts with her eyes "set in a fixed glare,"[133] and in Mary Grace who "scowls" into her book or has her eyes "fixed on Mrs. Turpin as if she had some very special reason for disliking her."[134] These frowning, disapproving expressions are used the same way in her cartoons as they are in her fiction. These reactions exaggerate and extend the comic effect of whatever statements or circumstances provoked them. They also invite a laugh at the display of ill humor that is part of the unfolding comedy.

This situation migrates almost unchanged to her fiction, with the exception that in her cartoons the scowl is usually part of the exchange between her favorite two girls, the short smart aleck and her tall, lanky companion. Her taste for comical pairings, however, remained with her. Hazel Motes and Enoch Emory in *Wise Blood*, Tarwater and Rayber in *The Violent Bear It Away*, Sally Poker Sash and the General in "A Late Encounter with The Enemy," Parker and Sarah-Ruth in "Parker's Back,"

and others like them can trace their lineage back to patterns established by O'Connor's two cartoon buddies. These characters in her fiction, like their cartoon predecessors, are actors in a comedy that shows neither one is as smart or as sophisticated as he thinks, and sometimes the fool gets the upper hand — a broad premise underlying her work that makes these characters laughable, and their struggles pathetic and human.

If pairing characters in her fiction is a distant cousin to her favorite cartoon scenario, her two buddies, there are at least a few characters that bear a closer resemblance to particular cartoons. The wallflower in glasses from "Oh, well, I can always be a Ph.D." is seen again in O'Connor's story "Good Country People" as the lady Ph.D. Hulga Hopewell. The punch line about the smart girl and her trouble getting a man is extended in this version as the reader follows Hulga's attempts to seduce a Bible salesman, Manly Pointer. It does not work out for her; he warns that "you needn't to think you'll catch me,"[135] as he runs off with her artificial leg in his suitcase. The angry girl with her book in "She says we're on the threshold of social revolution," from the April 5, 1945, *Colonnade*, re-emerges in the enraged Mary Grace in "Revelation," who hurls her copy of *Human Development* at Mrs. Turpin's head, hitting her just above the eye. The shock of that encounter vibrates in Mrs. Turpin till the story's conclusion, when her ideas about class and social order are turned upside down in a vision of blacks and white trash, freaks and lunatics ahead of her own kind in the procession of souls entering heaven.

Some of the scenarios O'Connor invented to dramatize in her fiction could work just as well as the basis of a cartoon, like Enoch Emory being insulted by a man in a gorilla suit in *Wise Blood*, Sally Poker Sash standing on the stage at the premier of *Gone With the Wind* with her brown Girl Scout shoes sticking out from under her evening gown, and a white woman meeting a black woman on the city bus wearing the same garish purple and green hat in "Everything that Rises Must Converge," which ends, of course, with one of them clobbering the other with her pocketbook. Bailey in "A Good Man Is Hard To Find," with his bald head and Hawaiian shirt, and the children's mother, whose face was "as broad and innocent as a cabbage" tied off with a green scarf that had "two points on the top like rabbit's ears,"[136] have all the appearance and substance of animated characters in a 1950s cartoon, complete with a couple of bratty comic-book-reading kids in the back seat of the car.

O'Connor had early on developed the habit of inventing characters and situations that would be suitable for a cartoon. In 1943, when she was describing to Hines how she came up with the ideas for her cartoons, she said first you had to catch your "rabbit" or good idea.[137] Then you had to tie it up someway with a situation or event. When she went hunting inspiration for her fiction, she was still looking in the same sorts of places and catching that same kind of rabbit — in the appearance and the behavior of the people around her, in an amusing gesture or statement, or in the lines of an article she read in the paper, like the one about a tattoo artist that inspired her story "Parker's Back."[138]

She didn't have a preconceived design and purpose for each cartoon; the process was more organic than that. She looked for something funny that she wanted to exploit without knowing what direction her creation would take or how it would become relevant to her audience. In "Writing Short Stories," O'Connor explains that the process a fiction writer goes through is similarly unplanned. When drafting "Good Country People," she didn't know she was going to write a story about a Ph.D. with a prosthetic leg: "I merely found myself one morning writing a description of two women that I knew something about, and before I realized it, I had equipped one of them with a daughter with a wooden leg."[139]

The beginning of her creative process for a story was similar to how she would have developed many of her cartoons. This does not mean the strategy was a deliberate exercise on her part. In describing how she wrote "Good Country People," she observes, "Technique works best when it is unconscious, and it was unconscious there."[140] The generative part of her process was closer to a habitual way of thinking, of conceiving, inventing, and describing characters and scenarios that she thought were funny. In her years as a cartoonist the process had become a well-traveled road that as a fiction writer she also followed as a reliable route to productivity. She slipped into its familiar grooves without having to think about it, and the story began to roll.

Whether it was two Jessies in raingear trekking across campus or two farm women standing in a kitchen talking, she started by sketching out a description of two women that she knew something about. O'Connor indicates that Mrs. Hopewell, the mother, is one of these characters. The other woman, the counterpart to Mrs. Hopewell, is Mrs. Freeman. And O'Connor begins her story with a description of her: "Besides the neutral expression that she wore when she was alone, Mrs. Freeman had two others, forward and reverse, that she used for all her human dealings."[141]

In O'Connor's cartoons, the facial expressions, though minimal, tell as much as the captions do about the scenario. They deliver the emotion and attitude of the response with a conciseness that words would not allow. Mrs. Freeman's "forward expression was steady and driving like the advance of a heavy truck."[142] In the backward expression, "her face came to a complete stop"[143] and her black eyes seemed to recede as she tries to avoid having to admit that she was wrong about something. Then O'Connor gives us a line for Mrs. Freeman to match the expression. "Well, I wouldn't of said it was, and I wouldn't of said it wasn't," she flaps. If O'Connor were drawing a cartoon, she'd be halfway there.

Before long, O'Connor has her duo exchanging some funny lines in a tit-for-tat competition in which Mrs. Freeman gives no headway to Mrs. Hopewell, who thinks of herself as the clever one:

> "Everybody is different," Mrs. Hopewell said.
> "Yes, most people is," Mrs. Freeman said.
> "It takes all kinds to make the world."
> "I always said it did myself."[144]

O'Connor appears to be following the pattern that she used for creating her cartoons of the two girls exchanging wise-cracks, one who thinks she's smart, the other, not so much, but there's a crucial variation. The frowning face one cartoon character usually offers in response to what her partner says is missing. Mrs. Freeman has her backward and forward expressions, and O'Connor allows her to deliver some telling glances with her "beady steel-pointed" eyes, but Mrs. Freeman is not the scowling girl. That girl comes into the picture as Mrs. Hopewell's daughter, Hulga, whose glum face and expressions of contempt are embroidered through the story. It's one of the reasons O'Connor needed her there, to be that disapproving observer, another of her favorite comic inventions. O'Connor begins to build her story around Hulga and gives her a comic foil in the form of a Bible salesman to complete another pairing. As the comedy plays out following her established pattern, the "smart" one becomes the fool in the end, teetering on the point of a pratfall, literally, without a leg to stand on.

The habits O'Connor developed as a cartoonist remained a creative resource for her. She was speaking from experience when she told novice fiction writers that stories don't start with an abstract idea, but with people and situations. The idea for a cartoon started in the same place. Whether her draft was composed of lines of text or the lines in a linoleum cut, she would return again and again to familiar scenarios and reliable bits of comedy to push the draft forward until it began to take on the shape of what it was to become. The regular work she did as a cartoonist, sketching comical images and creating captions for them, developed many of the habits and creative reflexes that would help her generate ideas for stories and plots, describe the appearance and behavior of characters, stage simple sequences, and compose some of those great one-liners readers love to memorize and repeat like the punch line for a joke every fan knows: "Shut up, Bobby Lee.... It's no real pleasure in life."[145]

When O'Connor asked to join the Writers' Workshop at Iowa, she wasn't starting from zero with fiction. Paul Engel might have made fun of her thick Southern drawl and her beat-up handbag, but when he read the writing samples she gave him, he found her stories "imaginative, tough, and alive."[146] She had written regular stories and satirical pieces for *The Corinthian* and also as part of her college course work. The number of cartoons she published and their wide appeal, however, might have given many who knew her then the impression that O'Connor was a cartoonist who also did some writing. How to resist the view of her now as a great writer who also did some cartoons?

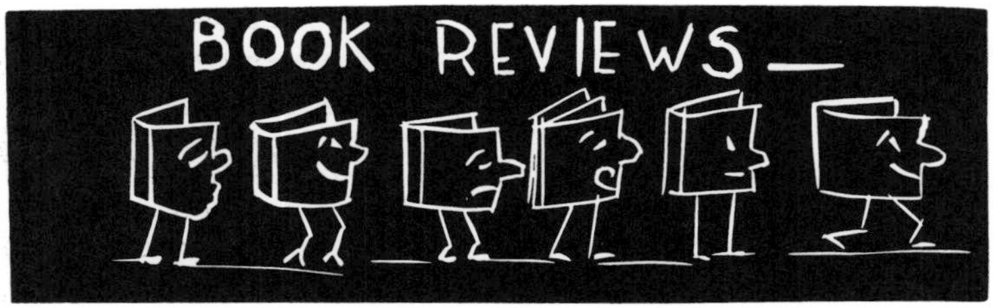
BOOK REVIEWS —

THE ROAD NOT TAKEN

From the years after her graduation from Iowa and up until the time her lupus was diagnosed, nothing much is known about her activity in the visual arts; yet, it seems that her interest in visual expression remained keen. In her adult life, especially during her time at Andalusia, she maintained her practice in the visual arts as a painter. She had an irrepressible talent for visual art, and she used the insights she gained from it to complement her fiction writing and, as she said, to have something to cover the walls. In her letters to friends she talked about painting, both what she was doing with hers and about painters whose work she admired. But she spoke of her work in the visual arts now mainly as a way of serving her fiction, and one result of this symbiosis is that some of the images she incorporated into her stories read like a canvas.

It could be an iconic image, like the one of Julian in "Everything that Rises Must Converge" rolling his eyes to heaven and "waiting like Saint Sebastian for the arrows to begin piercing him," or a modernist one, like the Cubist-inspired landscape of "black apartment buildings with irregular rectangles of light" rising up on either side of Julian and his mother at the end of the story, creating an atmosphere as empty and alienating as a city scene from an Edward Hopper painting.[147] Many of these painterly descriptions are seen in her treatment of the natural world, which was what she frequently painted at Andalusia, scenes from the farm and its surroundings. In "The Artificial Nigger," for example, she writes that "the sage grass was shivering gently in shades of silver and the clinkers under their feet glittered with a fresh black light. The treetops, fencing the junction like the protecting walls of a garden, were darker than the sky which was hung with gigantic white clouds illuminated like lanterns."[148] She narrates the scene as if she is describing a visual composition. Little wonder so many artists are inspired by O'Connor, finding in her prose images that become the subjects of their own paintings, prints, cartoons, or the inspiration for them.

The question still remains: Given that she had an active interest in continuing to work in the visual arts, why did she turn to painting after such a long and productive run as a cartoonist? Part of the answer may lie in her failure to find a publisher for her cartoons, other than the college in Milledgeville. However, she clearly had ambitions, sending them to *The New Yorker*, studying drawing in graduate school. As an undergraduate, she had once won a scholarship to an advertising art school in Nashville, though she didn't go,[149] and at GSCW she studied *A Century of Political Cartoons: Caricature in the United States from 1800 to 1900* published by Scribner's in 1944, rich with reproductions.[150] Trying her hand at a wartime cartoon in this genre resulted in a mother eagle criticizing a bomber dropping its payload in "Hrump — not enough pride to build a nest!" published in the April 19, 1945, *Colonnade*. Since she

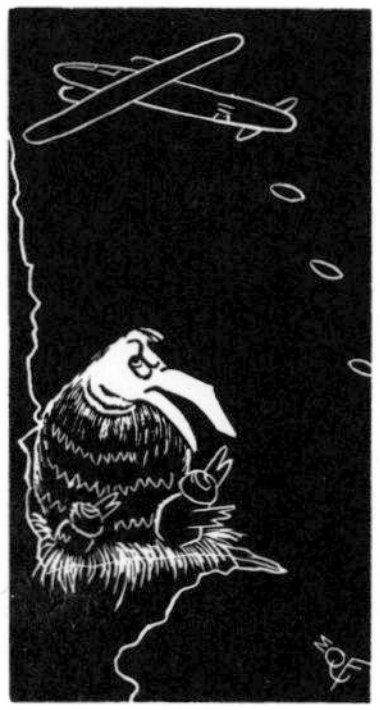

LEFT: *The Corinthian* (Winter 1943): 14. O'Connor created this decorative column header for the book reviews section of the publication. Her own tongue-in-cheek literary assessment of the children's classic *The Story of Ferdinand* by Munro Leaf appears among the reviews. "Stirring it its emotional appeal, exotic in its old-world background, and thoroughly significant in its similarity to predominating world conditions, *Ferdinand the Bull*, after only five years of circulation, has gained such a prominent position on college reading lists that it is now regarded by some educational and literary leaders as the sine qua non of the cultured mind," O'Connor proclaims.

was considering a career in journalism that combined work as a cartoonist, political cartooning was something she should be ready to show she could do, and do well.

Even when she got over her idea of being published in *The New Yorker* and submitted her work elsewhere, there were no takers. Perhaps she felt she was at a dead end with it, and needed to shift gears. If cartooning was married to the idea of a future in journalism, she was leaving all that behind to join the Writers' Workshop at Iowa. Through the workshop she acquired a fellowship from Rinehart Publishers in New York in 1947 to complete her first novel, *Wise Blood*, and she was once again on the path to publication and celebrity.

Part of the answer also may lie in how she felt her work as a cartoonist, or even identifying herself as a cartoonist, reflected her ambitions and her desire to be taken seriously. When she started writing fiction at Iowa, she decided to change her name. She seemed to think this would improve her chances of publication and get around any prejudices readers might have about her work when they saw "by Mary O'Connor" under the title line. "Who was likely to buy the stories of an Irish washer woman?" she complained.[151] She dropped her feminine first name and became Flannery O'Connor. In professional cartooning as in fiction writing, it was a man's world. And she didn't want to be mistaken for one of the tribe of drivel scribbling "pen women" she privately scorned while on the lecture circuit.

Aside from questions of gender bias, even the most successful cartoonists of the time, including Thurber, were dismissive of the idea that their work could be taken seriously. Helen Green said that she hoped O'Connor would not stop cartooning when she left GSCW, but "it was too light," she thought. "She was deeply serious."[152] "She knew Aquinas in detail, was amazingly well read in earlier philosophy, and developed into a first rate 'intellectual' along with her other accomplishments," wrote George Beiswanger, who came to GSCW in 1944 to be the chair of the art, philosophy, and religion departments. He had earned his Ph.D. from the University of Iowa and helped O'Connor secure a scholarship to go there. She impressed her fellow students at GSCW in a similar way. They thought of her as intellectually "far superior," "a brain," or simply "far out."[153]

There was only an inchoate conception in those days of how to combine fiction with cartooning; the graphic novel was a thing unknown, though her fiction became graphic in a way that admirers of that genre can appreciate. She did find, in painting, a way to pursue her passion for visual art without any lingering stigma. It was easy to dismiss a cartoonist's work as superficial; a painter, however, was a *real* artist. In addition to that consideration, cartooning is a far more social kind of activity; it requires an audience in a way that painting doesn't. A painter can work in isolation and still find satisfaction in what he produces, particularly if his livelihood is not dependent upon his art. But a cartoonist has a shared genealogy with performance art and composes with the expectation in mind that his work will be shared. Otherwise, it's like telling jokes to yourself when you're alone. There's just something missing.

When there was a particular recipient, O'Connor could not resist a cartoon here and there. In her letters to friends, she sometimes included drawings in the margins or inserted them between the lines of her text as if they were a natural extension of her writing. She added these for clarity, for emphasis, for sentiment, but mostly for fun. A few survive in letters to her closest friends, the ones for whom she knew the gesture wouldn't be out of place, fellow writer Maryat Lee and her college friend Betty Boyd Love. But mostly, her urge for cartooning had migrated to her fiction.

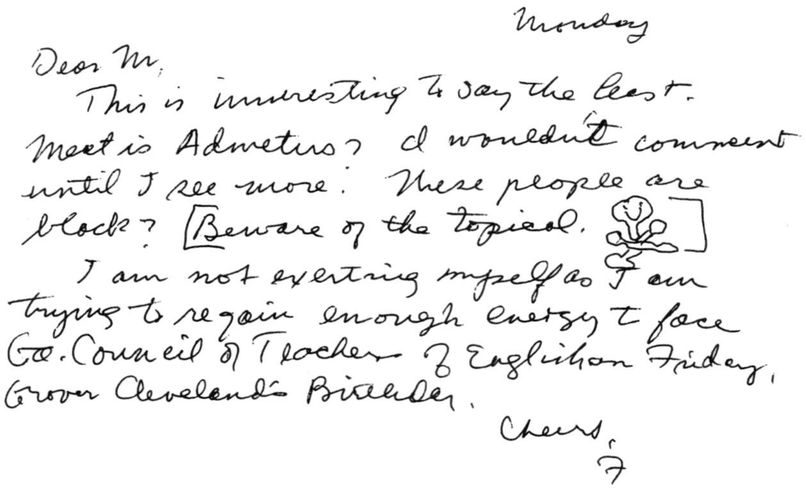
Monday

Dear M,

This is interesting to say the least. Meet is Admetus? I wouldn't comment until I see more. These people are black? [Beware of the topical.]

I am not exerting myself as I am trying to regain enough energy to face Ga. Council of Teachers of English on Friday, Grover Cleveland's Birthday.

Cheers,

F

RIGHT: O'Connor and Maryat Lee exchanged letters in March 1960 concerning some of Lee's work in progress. Lee was a prominent playwright on the street theater scene in New York City in the 1960s and founded SALT (Soul and Latin Theater) in East Harlem using untrained locals as actors. In one letter O'Connor asked, "These people are black?" and then warned her friend to "Beware of the topical" followed by the skull and crossbones drawing. [Special Collections, GCSU.]

In a 1959 letter to friend T. R. Spivey, O'Connor wrote that "15 to 18 is an age at which one is very sensitive to the sins of others, as I know from recollections of myself. At that age, you don't look for what is hidden."[154] Her satirical interest in the "sins" of others is abundantly evident in the cartoons she composed during her teens; her cartoons also seem to slide over the surface of things, with the artist happily mocking and mimicking her way through a two dimensional world.

As a young cartoonist, O'Connor had developed a sense of judgment all right, but it had not yet found its depth. As she redirected the full focus of her creativity into fiction writing at Iowa, she began to hunger to show how the characters and the scenarios she created could speak to something more profound. Her work migrated from a world of cartoon characters and gags to one of greater spiritual depth. The progression of her story lines sometimes follows this path as well, like the grandmother in "A Good Man Is Hard To Find" who only stops being a caricature at the point of a gun. Here the laughter stops and the drama becomes heartbreakingly real.

In a 1959 interview, O'Connor explained, "Mine is a comic art, but that does not detract from its seriousness."[155] She may have been taking a lesson from the master, Henry James, in forming this self-assessment. Her library contained a copy of a James monograph, "Daumier, Caricaturist," in which he praises the French artist and satirist Honoré Daumier, observing, "his comic force is serious" because it reflects "a strong sense of the nature of man."[156] For O'Connor, the deeper nature of mankind that she sounded became an expression of her faith. The anagogical vision she promoted, one that searched human experience for a more mysterious and profound spiritual meaning, applied as well to fiction. She advised other writers that "this enlarged view of the human scene" was what the writer had to cultivate "if he is ever going to write stories that have any chance of becoming a permanent part of our literature."[157]

The work of the artist, as she came to regard it, encompassed two of the most essential theological questions: What is the nature of the Divine? What is our relationship to it? Though the jokes still kept coming, the light-hearted and whimsical humor seen in her cartoons was often, in her fiction, drawn in more sinister tones. The journey grew darker and violent, evidence of the fallen state of humanity and the presence of evil in the world, as well as expressive of the mysteries of the Holy Spirit. The highly visual orientation of her prose took on other meanings, transforming into a language of signs and wonders. O'Connor was fond of telling people that anything that helps the writer to see helps his writing. A significant part of the experience she creates through her stories is also visual, with every reader, like the author herself, becoming a witness to the stranger truths her art reveals.

and I just
got back
yesterday

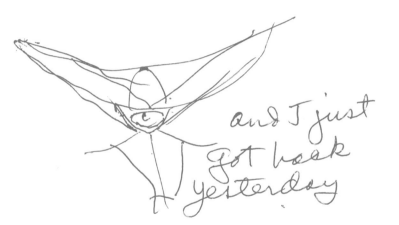

ABOVE: This illustration was included in a letter to Maryat Lee from November 1961 and was inserted into the body of O'Connor's text. She writes that she's been to St. Louis to lecture at a "college for all nuns — the kind that wear this kind of headgear" which she follows with the drawing. She completes the impression with "I just got back yesterday and they are all live wires."[Unpublished portion of letter to Maryat Lee, November 3, 1961. Special Collections, GCSU.] The nuns were all crazy about *The Violent Bear It Away*.

ENDNOTES

1 Jean Cash, *Flannery O'Connor: A Life* (Knoxville: University of Tennessee Press, 2002), 259.

2 Flannery O'Connor, "Writing Short Stories," *Mystery and Manners*, ed. Sally and Robert Fitzgerald (New York: Farrar, Straus and Cudahy, 1969), 91.

3 O'Connor, "The Nature and Aim of Fiction," *Mystery and Manners*, 84.

4 O'Connor, "Writing Short Stories," *Mystery and Manners*, 90.

5 Brad Gooch, *Flannery: A Life of Flannery O'Connor* (New York: Little, Brown and Company, 2009), 117.

6 Ibid., 54.

7 Barbara McKenzie, *Flannery O'Connor's Georgia* (Athens: University of Georgia Press, 1980), xvi.

8 Flannery O'Connor to Janet McKane, May 17, 1963, *The Habit of Being: Letters of Flannery O'Connor*, ed. Sally Fitzgerald (New York: Farrar, Straus and Giroux, 1979), 520.

9 O'Connor to William Sessions, July 8, 1956, *Habit of Being*, 164.

10 Gooch, *Flannery: A Life of Flannery O'Connor*, 33-34.

11 Ibid., 38.

12 Ibid., 27.

13 Ibid., 31, 33-34; Cash, *Flannery O'Connor: A Life*, 15.

14 McKenzie, *Flannery O'Connor's Georgia*, xviii.

15 Thea Jarvis, "Flannery – Georgia's Own," *The Atlanta Journal and Constitution*, May 8, 1980. Special Collections, GCSU.

16 Ibid.

17 Nelle Womack Hines, "Mary O'Connor Shows Talent as Cartoonist," *Macon Telegraph and News* (June 13, 1943): 3. Special Collections, GCSU.

18 Sally Fitzgerald, "Chronology" in *Flannery O'Connor: Collected Works*, ed. Sally Fitzgerald (New York: Library of America, 1988), 1,238.

19 Robert Fitzgerald, Introduction to *Everything that Rises Must Converge* by Flannery O'Connor, (New York: Farrar Straus and Giroux, 1965), xii.

20 Gooch, *Flannery: A Life of Flannery O'Connor*, 27.

21 O'Connor to Betty Hester, July 28, 1956, *Habit of Being*, 168.

22 Kathleen Feeley, S.S.N.D., "'Mine is a Comic Art...' Flannery O'Connor," *Realist of Distances: Flannery O'Connor Revisited*, ed. Karl Heinz Westarp and Jan Nordby Gretlund (Aarhus, Denmark: Aarus University Press, 1987), 67.

23 William Sessions, in discussion with the author, December 15, 2011. Sessions stated that a diary kept by Regina O'Connor indicates that mother and daughter were living in Milledgeville in January 1939 and that Flannery O'Connor may have been attending Peabody High School as early as the fall of 1938.

24 Chris Roberts, letter to the author, May 19, 1999. Roberts's paintings of "Uncle George" and Flannery O'Connor are inspired by Haslam's stories about O'Connor.

25 O'Connor to Betty Hester, August 11, 1956, *Habit of Being*, 169.

26 Gooch, *Flannery: A Life of Flannery O'Connor*, 75.

27 "Cartoon Girl," *The Alumnae Journal* (Spring 1944): 20.

28 *The Spectrum* (1944): 90. Special Collections, GCSU.

29 Cash, *Flannery O'Connor: A Life*, 22.

30 O'Connor, "The King of the Birds," *Mystery and Manners*, 4.

31 Ibid., 4.

32 O'Connor to Betty Hester, July 28, 1956, *Habit of Being*, 168.

33 Gooch, *Flannery: A Life of Flannery O'Connor*, 39.

34 Ibid., 34.

35 O'Connor, "The King of the Birds," *Mystery and Manners*, 4.

36 Cash, *Flannery O'Connor: A Life*, 45.

37 O'Connor to Betty Hester, June 14, 1958, *Habit of Being*, 288.

38 Cash, *Flannery O'Connor: A Life*, 43.

39 Ibid., 43.

40 Flannery O'Connor, "The Life You Save May Be Your Own," *Flannery O'Connor: Collected Works*, ed. Sally Fitzgerald (New York: Library of America, 1988), 173.

41 O'Connor, "Parker's Back," *Collected Works*, 660.

42 O'Connor, "The Displaced Person," *Collected Works*, 287.

43 O'Connor, *The Violent Bear It Away, Collected Works*, 462.

44 O'Connor, "The Enduring Chill," *Collected Works*, 572.

45 Flannery O'Connor, "Going to the Dogs," *The Corinthian* (Fall 1942): 14. Special Collections, GCSU.

46 Gooch, *Flannery: A Life of Flannery O'Connor*, 94.

47 "'What's in a Name?' Monogram Art," Paramount Pictures *Unusual Occupations* newsreel series, 1944.

48 Betty Boyd Love, "Recollections of Flannery O'Connor," *The Flannery O'Connor Bulletin* 14 (1985): 66.

49 Ibid., 64-71.

50 "College Sets Clocks Back," *The Colonnade* (January 30, 1943): 1. Special Collections, GCSU.

51 Cash, *Flannery O'Connor: A Life*, 61.

52 Ibid., 60.

53 Gooch, *Flannery: A Life of Flannery O'Connor*, 100.

54 O'Connor to Betty Hester, March 19, 1956, *Habit of Being*, 145.

55 Gooch, *Flannery: A Life of Flannery O'Connor*, 116.

56 Hines, "Mary O'Connor Shows Talent as Cartoonist," 3.

57 Gooch, *Flannery: A Life of Flannery O'Connor*, 55.

58 Ibid., 99.

59 John McCabe, *Mr. Laurel and Mr. Hardy* (London: Robinson Books, 1976), 67.

60 Quoted in McCabe, *Mr. Laurel and Mr. Hardy*, 68.

61 Alfie Geeson, "Oliver Hardy: The Unveiling of a Oliver Hardy Commemorative Plaque," *Fucia Land*, accessed May 1, 2011. http://www.fuchsialand.co.uk/oliver/oliver.htm.

62 Mary Brewton, "Broodings: Jimmies May Be Proud but So Are Jessies," *The Colonnade* (May 2, 1944): 2. Special Collections, GCSU.

63 O'Connor to Betty Hester, June 28, 1956, *Habit of Being*, 163-64.

64 Love, "Recollections of Flannery O'Connor," 65.

65 O'Connor to Betty Hester, April 13, 1963, *Habit of Being*, 513.

66 Ibid., 513.

67 Quoted in Gooch, *Flannery: A Life of Flannery O'Connor*, 90.

68 Ibid., 91.

69 Ibid., 91.

70 Quoted in Hines, "Mary O'Connor Shows Talent as Cartoonist," 3.

71 Gooch, *Flannery: A Life of Flannery O'Connor*, 73-74.

72 Quoted in Gooch, *Flannery: A Life of Flannery O'Connor*, 110.

73 Fitzgerald, Introduction to *Everything That Rises Must Converge*, xii.

74 Ibid., xii.

75 "Art: Artists in Residence," *Time*, September 23, 1940, http://www.time.com/time/magazine/article/0,9171,801997,00.html.

76 Lothar Hönnighausen, *William Faulkner: The Art of Stylization in His Early Graphic and Literary Work* (New York: Cambridge University Press, 1987), 53-55.

77 John Held, Jr., "There was a dark form at the other end of the bench," reprinted in "It was the Jazz Age and John Held, Jr. Drew It and Lived It" by Dorothy and John Tarrant, *Smithsonian* 17.6 (1986): 94-105.

78 Carol Jean Cason, "Alumnae Adventuring," *The Alumnae Journal* (Fall 1948): 11.

79 Helen I. Greene, "Mary Flannery O'Connor: One Teacher's Happy Memory," *The Flannery O'Connor Bulletin* 19 (1990): 45.

80 Cash, *Flannery O'Connor: A Life*, 72.

81 Dorothy Parker, Preface to *James Thurber's Men, Women, and Dogs* by James Thurber (New York: Harcourt, Brace and Company,1943), ix.

82 O'Connor, "Going to the Dogs," 14.

83 James Thurber, *Thurber and Company* (New York: Harper and Row Publishers, 1966), 104-105.

84 "Art: Men, Women, and Dogs," review of *James Thurber's Men Women and Dogs* by James Thurber, *Time*, November 15, 1943, http://www.time.com/time/magazine/article/0,9171,885210,00.html#ixzz1N0zVq1IT.

85 "College Aims Rejuvenated," *The Colonnade* (January 2, 1943): 4. Special Collections, GCSU.

86 "O'Connor, Sperry, Anderson Honored," *The Colonnade* (April 5, 1945): 1. Special Collections, GCSU.

87 O'Connor to Janet McKane, August 27, 1963, *Habit of Being*, 536.

88 Eudora Welty, letter to *The New Yorker*, 1933, quoted in "A Job for Eudora Welty" by Macy Halford. New Yorker Book Bench Blog, April 12, 2011, http://www.newyorker.com/online/blogs/books/2011/04/a-job-for-eudora-welty.html.

89 O'Connor, "The Fiction Writer and His Country," *Mystery and Manners*, 34.

90 "Orchestra and Music Club Organized," *The Peabody Palladium* (October 28, 1940): 1. Special Collections, GCSU.

91 Cash, *Flannery O'Connor: A Life*, 42.

92 Ibid., 42.

93 "Journalism Class Edits Palladium," *The Peabody Palladium*, (December 18, 1940): 1. Special Collections, GCSU.

94 "Snooped Scoops," *The Peabody Palladium* (December 12, 1941): 3. Special Collections, GCSU.

95 Fran Richardson, quoted in Gooch, *Flannery: A Life of Flannery O'Connor*, 86.

96 "Keeping Fit: Physical Fitness Program to be Daily Feature at GSCW," *The Colonnade* (October 9, 1942): 3. Special Collections, GCSU.

97 Jewell Willie, "Oh, How We Hate To Get Up The Week After Being Fit," *The Colonnade* (October 9, 1942): 4. Special Collections, GCSU.

98 William Ivy Hair, et al., *A Centennial History of Georgia College* (Milledgeville, Georgia College: 1979), 182.

99 "Frosh Bow to Mighty Sophs In Annual Slipper Contest" *The Colonnade* (November 14, 1942): 1. Special Collections, GCSU.

100 Ibid., 1.

101 Ibid., 1.

102 "Dispassionate Shepard" *The Colonnade* (May 22, 1943): 2. Special Collections, GCSU.

103 "...two more weeks (plus three days) we won't be a-doin' this..." *The Spectrum* (1944):132. Special Collections, GCSU.

104 "CGA and Art Department Will Sponsor Exhibition: Display of Works of Modern Artists Slated for January 15-19 in Library," *The Colonnade* (January 2, 1943):1. Special Collections, GCSU.

105 "Art Exhibition in Second Week," *The Colonnade* (January 9, 1943): 3. Special Collections, GCSU.

106 Hazel Smith, "Campus Fashions," *The Colonnade* (November 21, 1942): 4. Special Collections, GCSU.

107 Quoted in Gooch, *Flannery: A Life of Flannery O'Connor*, 95.

108 Flannery O'Connor, "Fashion's Perfect Medium," *The Corinthian* (Fall 1944): 12. Special Collections, GCSU.

109 Joyce Moncrief, "You Can Have My Share," *The Corinthian* (Fall 1944): 14. Special Collections, GCSU.

110 Ibid., 14.

111 O'Connor, "The Comforts of Home," *Collected Works*, 573.

112 "Welcome Parents and Friends," *The Colonnade* (October 17, 1942): 4. Special Collections, GCSU.

113 "LATE FLASH," *The Colonnade* (October 17, 1942): 1. Special Collections, GCSU.

114 Quoted in Hair et al., *A Centennial History of Georgia College*, 216.

115 Hair et al., *A Centennial History of Georgia College*, 215.

116 Quoted in Gooch, *Flannery: A Life of Flannery O'Connor*, 97.

117 O'Connor, "The Nature and Aim of Fiction," *Mystery and Manners*, 77.

118 Quoted in Cash, *Flannery O'Connor: A Life*, 61.

119 Hair et al., *A Centennial History of Georgia College*, 208.

120 "Bob Hope Entertains Navy Tonight; Students Invited to Attend Program," *The Colonnade* (May 15, 1943): 1. Special Collections, GCSU.

121 Feeley, "Mine is a Comic Art," 67.

122 *The Spectrum* (1944): 90. Special Collections, GCSU.

123 O'Connor's University of Iowa transcript indicates she took advanced drawing during her first and second semesters. She also took a course in advertising during her first semester. Special Collections, GCSU.

124 Gooch, *Flannery: A Life of Flannery O'Connor*, 120.

125 O'Connor to Ben Griffith, June 8, 1955, *Habit of Being*, 83.

126 O'Connor, "Revelation," *Collected Works*, 637.

127 O'Connor, "Everything That Rises Must Converge," *Collected Works*, 490.

128 Ibid., 492.

129 Gooch, *Flannery: A Life of Flannery O'Connor*, 31.

130 Loretta Feuger Hoynes, quoted in Cash, *Flannery O'Connor: A Life*, 48.

131 O'Connor, "A Good Man Is Hard to Find," *Collected Works*, 208.

132 O'Connor, "A Circle in the Fire," *Collected Works*, 238 and 247.

133 O'Connor, "Everything That Rises Must Converge," *Collected Works*, 546.

134 Ibid., 638.

135 O'Connor, "Good Country People," *Collected Works*, 283.

136 O'Connor, "A Good Man Is Hard to Find," *Collected Works*, 137.

137 Hines, "Mary O'Connor Shows Talent as Cartoonist," 3.

138 James F. Farnham, "Further Evidence for the Sources of 'Parker's Back,'" *The Flannery O'Connor Bulletin* 12 (1983): 114-116.

139 O'Connor, "Writing Short Stories," *Mystery and Manners*, 100.

140 O'Connor to Betty Hester, August 24, 1956, *Habit of Being*, 171.

141 O'Connor, "Good Country People," *Collected Works*, 263.

142 Ibid., 263.

143 Ibid., 263.

144 Ibid., 265.

145 Ibid., 153.

146 Quoted in Gooch, *Flannery: A Life of Flannery O'Connor*, 118.

147 O'Connor, "Everything That Rises Must Converge," *Collected Works*, 485 and 499.

148 O'Connor, "A Circle in the Fire," *Collected Works*, 230.

149 Elizabeth Shreve Ryan, "I Remember Mary Flannery," *The Flannery O'Connor Bulletin* 19 (1990): 51.

150 Gooch, *Flannery: A Life of Flannery O'Connor*, 110.

151 Quoted in Richard Gilman, "On Flannery O'Connor," *New York Review of Books* (August 21, 1969): 24.

152 Quoted in Cash, *Flannery O'Connor: A Life*, 61.

153 Ibid., 58.

154 O'Connor to T.R. Spivey, August 19, 1959, *Habit of Being*, 346.

155 Betsy Lochridge, "An Afternoon with Flannery O'Connor," *The Atlanta Journal and Constitution* (November 1, 1955): 38-40.

156 Quoted in Feeley, "Mine is a Comic Art," 70-71.

157 O'Connor, "The Nature and Aim of Fiction," *Mystery and Manners*, 73.

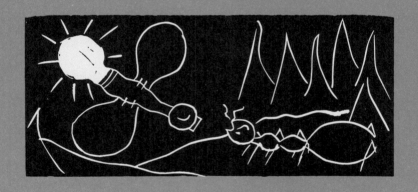

ART CREDITS

THE PEABODY PALLADIUM was the student newspaper of Peabody High School. O'Connor regularly contributed cartoons to the paper and became its art editor in October 1940. Peabody High School was part of the Peabody Practice School, where education majors at Georgia State College for Women received their practical training and were mentored by GSCW professors.

PAGE 3, LEFT "One Result of the New Peabody Orchestra," *The Peabody Palladium* (October 28, 1940): 2. A front page article in this issue announced the organization of a new orchestra and music club.

PAGE 3, RIGHT "Thanksgiving," *The Peabody Palladium* (November 20, 1940): 1. This cartoon was an illustration for the article "Dr. Oakey Talks at Wednesday Morning Thanksgiving Service." Oakey was the pastor of the Milledgeville Presbyterian Church. The program included a devotional, a play, a display of food baskets for the needy donated by students, and concluded with the hymn "Father, We Thank Thee."

PG 5L "Just One More Day To Dream," *The Peabody Palladium* (November 20, 1940): 2. O'Connor's review of *My Mother Is a Violent Woman* by Tommy Wadelton and her poem "The First Book" were also published on this page, above and to the left of her cartoon.

PG 5R "'Twas the Night Before Press Time," *The Peabody Palladium* (December 18, 1940): 2. This issue of the *Palladium* was edited as a class project by the junior-level journalism class in which O'Connor was likely a student. The paper also proudly announced its membership in the Georgia Scholastic Press Association, beginning with this issue.

PG 7L "The Wrong Way To Do It," *The Peabody Palladium* (February 21, 1941): 2. "Council Room Is Decorated," an article on page four of this issue, noted that Mary Patrick and Lillian Arnold, who were involved in the redecorating, had laundered all of the chair covers. They would have welcomed O'Connor's additional instruction to students.

PG 7R "Senior, Senior, Wherefore Art Thou, Senior?" *The Peabody Palladium* (March 21, 1941): 2. "Seniors Present Annual Plays," an article on the front page, announced the theatricals to be held the following Friday night. In the junior class plays staged the week before this cartoon was published, O'Connor performed the part of "Mr. Lacy" and her friend Elizabeth Shreve was "Izzie Wiffle" in a play titled "Sardines."

PG 9L "Now Comes Spring Fever," *The Peabody Palladium* (April 25, 1941): 2. On page three of this issue, there's some indication of what the mostly female students at Peabody High School were dreaming about, the new spring fashions: "In the spring a young man's fancy lightly turns to thoughts of love, while a young lady's fancy turns to thoughts of clothes." O'Connor's daydream visions have a different focus.

PG 9R "At Long Last . . ." *The Peabody Palladium* (May 23, 1941): 2. The school term ended on May 30 that year, but graduation exercises were held for seniors a day earlier, on May 29.

PG 11L "In Hopes That a Jimmie Soon Will Be There," *The Peabody Palladium* (December 12, 1941): 2. "Jimmie" was the nickname for students attending Georgia Military College located near GSCW in Milledgeville. Most Jimmies were high school students and would soon be enlisting to serve in World War II.

PG 11R "Music Appreciation Hath Charms," *The Peabody Palladium*, circa 1942. This cartoon was republished by *The Flannery O'Connor Bulletin* in 1990 from a clipping provided by Elizabeth Shreve Ryan. Peabody High School offered an elective "Music Appreciation Hour" one morning each week. Students selected the records, and the playlist and other details about the program were regularly reported in the *Palladium*.

PG 13 "These Two Express the Universal Feeling of Heart-Brokenness Over School Closing," *The Peabody Palladium*, circa 1942. This cartoon was republished by *The Flannery O'Connor Bulletin* in 1990 from a clipping provided by Elizabeth Shreve Ryan.

THE COLONNADE was the student newspaper for GSCW. George Haslam, a journalism professor at the college and the advisor for *The Peabody Palladium* and *The Colonnade*, encouraged O'Connor's contributions to both papers. Her cartoons began to run in *The Colonnade* in the fall of 1942. She became art editor of *The Colonnade* in March 1943 and was a regular contributor until her graduation in 1945. *The Colonnade* was a weekly publication from 1942 to 1943. In the fall of 1943, the newspaper converted to bi-monthly publication due to reduced enrollment and paper shortages during World War II.

PG 15L "The Immediate Results of Physical Fitness Day," *The Colonnade* (October 9, 1942): 4. Jewell Willie's article "Oh, How We Hate To Get Up The Week After Being Fit," published with O'Connor's cartoon on page four, describes the aftereffects of the school's exercise program as "torture of inquisitional intensity": "Every muscle in our collective anatomies was corroded by every fatigue acid ever invented. We behaved like homing pigeons every time we beheld a pillow – or even a chair."

PG 15R "Why Don't We Do This More Often?" *The Colonnade* (October 17, 1942): 4. Two articles published alongside the cartoon document GSCW's fourth annual Parents' Day. Lunch was served on the front campus lawn to students and their visitors as part of the event.

PG 17L "Aw nuts, I thought we'd have at least one day off after the faculty played softball!" *The Colonnade* (October 24, 1942): 4. A front-page story about the annual hike to Treanor's Meadow, "'Jessies' Dash Back from Hike as Rain Catches Them," reports that "the faculty gained a 13 to 12 victory over the seniors in a 'neck and neck' softball game, due to a great extent, no doubt, to Dr. Wells' wicked curve ball." Guy H. Wells was the college's president from 1934 to 1953.

PG 17R "Oh, gosh! I didn't know you had to pay a poll tax." *The Colonnade* (November 7, 1942): 4. "Dormitory Officers Elected Last Week" announced the election results on the first page of the following issue of *The Colonnade*, published November 14.

PG 19L "Doggone this Golden Slipper Contest. Now we have to wear saddle oxfords." *The Colonnade* (November 14, 1942): 4. "Frosh Bow to Mighty Sophs In Annual Slipper Contest," published on the front page, reported the outcome of GSCW's annual drama competition. The trophy, an ornamental golden slipper, was traded back and forth between the winning classes each year.

PG 19R "Term Papers Add Quite a Lot to These Thanksgiving Holidays," *The Colonnade* (November 21, 1942): 4.

PG 21L "Are you glad to be back?" *The Colonnade* (December 5, 1942): 4. Following the Thanksgiving holiday, freshmen returned to undergo the trials of Rat Day, a day of hazing in which the junior class forced the freshmen to do chores and follow random commands. Freshmen who refused to obey were sent to Rat Court for a mock trial at the end of the day. O'Connor was supposedly sentenced to wear an onion around her neck, which she refused to do.

PG 21R "In the light of our common knowledge, don't you consider this examination business rather superfluous?" *The Colonnade* (December 12, 1942): 4.

PG 23L "Business as Usual," *The Colonnade* (January 2, 1943): 4. "College Aims Rejuvenated," an article published next to the cartoon on this page, provides another layer to O'Connor's satire about the effects of wartime rationing when it proclaims: "As a new quarter and a new year's beginning, we now have an opportunity to 'pull in our belts' and determine that our men in service shall not do all of the fighting."

PG 23R "Aw, don't worry about not getting on the Dean's List. It's no fun going to the picture show at night anyway." *The Colonnade* (January 9, 1943): 4. An article on the front page listed eighty students who had qualified for the Dean's List for the fall quarter. For the first and only time during her years at GSCW, O'Connor's name was not on the list.

PG 25L "I don't enjoy looking at these old pictures either, but it doesn't hurt my reputation for people to think I'm a lover of fine arts." *The Colonnade* (January 16, 1943): 4. For several weeks in January, the college hosted an exhibit that included reproductions of works by Van Gogh, Daumier, Corot, and Cézanne, among others. On page three of this issue, a short list of students' favorite paintings was published, along with the news that 333 students had signed the exhibit guest register.

PG 25R "Officer or no officer, I'm going to ask her to let me try on that hat." *The Colonnade* (January 23, 1943): 4. "Fifteen WAVE Officials Arrive Here to Prepare for Training Center," an article on the first page of this issue, notes the arrival of Navy officers prior to launching the WAVES school at GSCW during World War II.

PG 27L "But I tell you, you don't have to get a rooster to tell when to get up; all you have to do is set your clock back." *The Colonnade* (January 30, 1943): 4. In this issue, GSCW announced its change from Eastern Standard War time to Central Standard War time, setting the clocks and the school's schedule back by one hour.

PG 27R "Now why waste all your energy getting physically fit? You'll never look like a WAVE anyhow." *The Colonnade* (February 6, 1943): 4. Photos of WAVES marching in formation appeared in this issue, along with reports of an aggressive fitness program for students. The chairman of the Physical Fitness Committee reported that up to ninety percent of GSCW's students were participating in nightly exercises in the dormitories. A WAVES recruiting message was published parallel to O'Connor's cartoon on page four.

PG 29L "Traffic," *The Colonnade* (February 13, 1943): 4. The WAVES training regimen required sixteen miles of marching every day, and students often had to make way for the columns of WAVES marching in formation across campus. The crowding caused by the WAVES school at GSCW was the source of some grumbling, but the college students were also proud of the sacrifices they were making to support the war effort.

PG 29R "See there, I told you they didn't keep gunpowder in those things." *The Colonnade* (February 20, 1943): 4. While GSCW's students and the WAVES generally didn't mix, special events were occasionally arranged to bring them together, such as a basketball game between GSCW seniors and the WAVES reported in "Seniors Sing Navy," on page two of this issue.

PG 31L "It's a shame nobody petitioned me for an office. I could have done much more for Faculty-Student relations." *The Colonnade* (February 27, 1943): 4. This issue of *The Colonnade* reported election results for various student organizations. One letter from a student published on the same page as this cartoon reminds new officers of their responsibility to the student body, another complains of the lack of student participation in the recent elections. The Faculty-Student Relations Committee was concerned with the rules maintained by GSCW faculty for the school's resident students.

PG 31R "Oh, give me back my raincoat; you still look more like a moron than a WAVE." *The Colonnade* (March 6, 1943): 4. Graduation for the first class of WAVES was scheduled for March 15, and several articles published in this issue anticipate that event. It seemed to rain a lot in Milledgeville, and O'Connor frequently depicted students in raingear.

PG 33L "Coming back affects some people worse than others." *The Colonnade* (March 20, 1943): 2. "New Wardrobe and Sulphur-Molasses Vie for First Place on Campus," an article published next to O'Connor's cartoon on this page, describes students returning from spring break: "Bunny hugs and shrill screams beckoned in spring quarter, as vacation-revived Jessies again flooded the campus." This issue of *The Colonnade* also announced that GSCW was flooded by 400 new WAVES.

PG 33R "Targets Are Where You Find 'Em!" *The Colonnade* (March 27, 1943): 2. "400 More Waves Expected in July; Junior Colleges May be Dropped," an article on page three opposite O'Connor's cartoon, addresses the difficulties colleges face when flooded by armed forces training and regular student enrollment.

PG 35L "Oh, well, I can always be a Ph.D." *The Colonnade* (April 3, 1943): 2. An article positioned directly above the cartoon, "Them's What Has 'Em Entertain 'Em," discusses opening the gym on Saturday and Sunday so that students could entertain visitors, because, as its author claims: "Students who get dates deserve help in entertaining them."

PG 35R "I think it's perfectly idiotic of the Navy not to let you WAVES dress sensibly like us college girls." *The Colonnade* (April 10, 1943): 2. "Play Night Reinaugurated; As Need Arises on Campus Group and Individual Games Offered: 100 WAVES Invited Each Week," an article on the front page of this issue, describes a weekly event providing GSCW students, WAVES, and their dates with an opportunity to dance and socialize in the gym.

PG 37L "Wake me up in time to clap!" *The Colonnade* (April 17, 1943): 2. This cartoon illustrated the article "Wake Me Up In Time to Clap!" which offered a student perspective on the chapel program: "Among the many little burdensome activities involved in college life, the chapel program is the most conducive to general student insanity. The difficulties one may encounter in preserving the disposition, home training and moral equilibrium while sitting through such an affair can be appreciated only by those who have suffered, in particularly by those who have suffered quietly."

PG 37R "If we moved all those hats on the wrong hooks, do you think we'd still be eligible for the Dean's List?" *The Colonnade* (April 24, 1943): 2. O'Connor did make the Dean's List that spring, but the list wasn't published in *The Colonnade* till the following fall.

PG 39L "Aw, quit trying to tell me that thing means she's a *messenger*. I'm not so dumb." *The Colonnade* (May 15, 1943): 2. The WAVES school at GSCW was large enough to attract entertainer Bob Hope. A headline in this issue announces: "Bob Hope Entertains Navy Tonight; Students Invited to Attend Program." His radio show was broadcast coast-to-coast from the campus on May 18, 1943.

PG 39R "Those are the kind of WAVES I like." *The Colonnade* (May 22, 1943): 2. The column "Dispassionate Shepard," published directly below this cartoon, describes a scene from a campus mixer: "Will you ever forget how gladly the WAVES and Marines welcomed our friendly advances at our joint picnic supper on the front campus?" The scarcity of young men in Milledgeville during the war years caused some students to dub the school "Georgia State College for Wallflowers."

PG 41L "Gosh, we're glad to be back." *The Colonnade* (September 28, 1943): 2. The column "Dispassionate Shepard," published directly below this cartoon, discusses students' low spirits upon return to campus after the summer break. *The Colonnade* also announced in this issue that it would be published bi-monthly during the school year, instead of weekly, due to the wartime paper shortage and decreased enrollment.

PG 41R "Do you think teachers are necessary?" *The Colonnade* (October 5, 1943): 2.

PG 43L "They are giving us entirely too much work. Why, I don't have time for but six outside activities!" *The Colonnade* (October 19, 1943): 2. The process of nominating and electing new officers for student organizations was in full swing when this issue was published, but "Advice to Freshmen," an article that ran on the front page of the previous *Colonnade*, on October 5, was more to the point: "Organizations are always wary of those of you who contract 'joining fever.' Join more than one

organization if you wish, but try to keep them limited to those you know you're interested in, and skip the ones you just think you're interested in."

PG 43R "Could I interest you in buying a Contemporary Georgia syllabus?" *The Colonnade* (November 9, 1943): 2. O'Connor majored in Social Science rather than English in order to avoid a teacher who had given her low grades in writing. According to biographer Brad Gooch, O'Connor's cartoon commentary on Social Science 200, Contemporary Georgia Problems, shows that the trade-off wasn't always an appealing solution.

PG 45L "Just the thought of getting away from here for a few days unhinges some people, you know." *The Colonnade* (November 23, 1943): 2. The column "Brewton's Broodings," published directly above the cartoon, recommends a few bizarre pranks to lift students' pre-Thanksgiving holiday blues, including staging your own funeral and introducing a store mannequin as your mother.

PG 45R "I wonder if there could be anything to that business about studying at the first of the quarter?" *The Colonnade* (December 14, 1943): 2. "Procrastination is Dissipation," an article published on the same page as this cartoon, offers its insights a bit late for students taking final exams in the next few days.

PG 47L "I hear there's a shortage of classrooms." *The Colonnade* (January 4, 1944): 2. The crowding and competition for college resources caused by the WAVES school at GSCW is O'Connor's subject. In her column "Brooding," published on the same page as O'Connor's cartoon, Mary Brewton expresses the frustrations of many students as she carps about her New Year's resolution: "Oh, well, it is a new year and I might as well start right now not griping about things."

PG 47R "This Can Never Be Done in Ten Minutes," *The Colonnade* (January 18, 1944): 2. Published directly below O'Connor's cartoon in this issue, an open letter from the Scholarship Committee includes a list of problems that prevent students from being more enthusiastic and successful in their studies at GSCW, such as excessive noise in the dorms and improper distribution of time. "With the elimination of these hindrances," the committee reported, "would come a new growth of interest."

PG 49L "Two mo' monts we won' be a-doin' it..." *The Colonnade* (February 1, 1944): 2. In addition to anticipating the upcoming spring break, this cartoon appears to have captured some of the lines that the WAVES would sing or chant as they marched. It also may be intended to recall the students who showed up in blackface at the Golden Slipper Contest the year before. Adding a particular note of irony to the cartoon is Mary Boyd's article "The Good Old Days … Or Why Parents Have Grey Hair," which appeared above O'Connor's carton on this page. Boyd reminds students that they came to college to work hard and make good, so "your folks would be proud of you."

PG 49R "Kilpatrick was fair." *The Colonnade* (February 15, 1944): 2. William Heard Kilpatrick, a Georgia native and student of John Dewey, developed the Project Method for early childhood education which was supported by a philosophy of experience-centered learning guided by students' interests. This issue announced that Kilpatrick would visit the campus to speak to students on February 18 and 19. The education department at GSCW was deeply influenced by his pedagogy.

PG 51L "I believe the totalitarian outlook of the aggressive minority in the educational-governmental faction should be crushed, and if I am elected sixth vice recording secretary, I shall bend every effort to crush it." *The Colonnade* (February 29, 1944): 2. Elections for student government were particularly heated in 1944 as students' complaints about the strict rules governing resident student life peaked after the state lowered the voting age to eighteen. O'Connor's friend Betty Boyd was one of those running for office and would be elected president of the College Government Association, in addition to reporting for various campus committees.

PG 51R "I hope the rules of that place slacken up before we start going out with girls." *The Colonnade* (March 7, 1944): 2. Increased freedom and autonomy for GSCW's resident students were prevailing themes for student government elections in 1944. A common platform described in an article introducing the candidates on page two of this issue: "Dates anytime, anybody, anywhere."

PG 53L "Madam Chairman, the committee has reached a decision." *The Colonnade* (April 4, 1944): 2. The usual four-page *Colonnade* was expanded to six pages to accommodate extended reporting on the shake-up in student government at GSCW that year. Among the many committees reporting in this issue were the Scholarship Committee, War Service Committee, Fine Arts Committee, Honor Committee, Executive Committee, and the Good Manners Committee.

PG 53R "Counter-Attack," *The Colonnade* (April 18, 1944): 2. O'Connor was a member of the International Relations Club, which summarized news from the European and Pacific theaters in its column published next to her cartoon. On the facing page, the article "Washington Complains that Women Are Unprofessional" describes a government administrator's prejudice against hiring women because of the quarrelsome behavior among his female staff.

PG 55L "The whole family's been wintering here at GSCW — you have to take what you can get these days." *The Colonnade* (May 2, 1944): 2. In her column for this issue, Carla Ogletree considers where students will be going after the spring term ends: "Summer for some of us means a couple of months in a camp in Vermont or maybe Virginia. For all it means new coats of color, and frequent plunges at a beach or in some blue, blue pool."

PG 55R "This place will never amount to anything until they get a Student Committee on Faculty Relations." *The Colonnade* (May 23, 1944): 2. "Faculty-Student Relations Committee Passes New CGA Constitutional Changes, Rules" was headline news in this issue. The faculty had agreed to relax some of the rules governing student conduct, including allowing students to ride in cars with boys before 6:00 p.m., come to breakfast on Sundays with their hair in rollers, and walk anywhere in town with their dates, except for certain restricted areas and the cemetery.

PG 57L "It breaks my heart to leave for a whole summer." *The Colonnade* (May 30, 1944): 2. In addition to marking the end of the spring quarter and the beginning

of summer break, O'Connor appears to be toying with a representation of the Solemnity of the Ascension of the Lord, an iconic image in Christian art with the resurrected Christ rising into the air amid astonished or enraptured onlookers.

PG 57R "I understand it's a form of physic maladjustment created by a marked dissatisfaction with a change in environment wherein the family unit is disrupted — called homesickness." *The Colonnade* (September 26, 1944): 2.

PG 59L "Now if 50,000 paratyphoid bacillae can go through the eye of a needle abreast, that ought to put at least 500,000,000,000 in that spoonful; and you should be ill by early tomorrow morning." *The Colonnade* (October 10, 1944): 2. That fall, a food poisoning epidemic at GSCW, with 140 documented cases in a ten-day period, caused a serious scare. "Para-B Typhoid Crisis Alleviated," an article on page one of this issue, reports: "All food sources were examined by the health department and it recommended that certain cooks in the Atkinson dining hall be removed. The food service was reorganized to eliminate all possible sources of the germs."

PG 59R "Understand, I got nothing against getting educated, but it just looks like there ought to be an easier way to do it." *The Colonnade* (October 24, 1944): 2. O'Connor made front-page news in this issue in "Twelve Seniors Selected for 1944-45 Who's Who." Among the selected twelve, O'Connor was listed with the following credentials: "editor of *Corinthian*, art editor of *Colonnade*, member of IRC [International Relations Club]."

PG 61L "I demand an honorary organization for the C-Group!" *The Colonnade* (November 18, 1944): 2. In the previous issue of *The Colonnade*, on October 24, the creation of a new honorary group was announced for sophomores with a "B" average.

PG 61R "...and I ask you — how many Pilgrim Fathers had to write term-papers during Thanksgiving." *The Colonnade* (December 6, 1944): 4.

PG 63L "Do you have any books the faculty doesn't particularly recommend?" *The Colonnade* (January 24, 1945): 4. Students who visited the library earlier in the winter quarter were asked to complete a survey. The results were later reported in "Library Questionnaire Helps Ferret Out Pet Peeves of Studious Jessies" in the February 22, 1945, *Colonnade*. Along with requests for the library to improve its book selection, the questionnaire showed that most students were "interested in studying and in better study conditions."

PG 63R "I understand she says it's the happy way of doing things." *The Colonnade* (February 7, 1945): 4. According to biographer Brad Gooch, one of O'Connor's professors, George Beiswanger, provided the occasion for this cartoon when he opened his first lecture to the student body, arranged by the Good Manners Committee, with this quote from Ralph Waldo Emerson: "Manners are the happy way of doing things."

PG 65L *The Colonnade* (February 22, 1945): 4. In addition to the International Relations Club's column "The War This Week," a notice encouraging the purchase of war bonds was published adjacent to O'Connor's WAVES cartoon in this issue, reminding readers: "Your opportunity to show your faith in your country will come soon. Don't be caught napping."

PG 65R *The Colonnade* (March 7, 1945): 4. A construction project on the front campus that spring had students navigating a series of large holes and temporary walkways. "Give Till It Hurts!" was the headline directly below O'Connor's cartoon. It was an announcement encouraging students to donate to the Red Cross that week; the goal was one dollar for every student.

PG 67L "She says we're on the threshold of social revolution." *The Colonnade* (April 5, 1945): 4. "It's Your World — Know It," an article published directly above O'Connor's cartoon on this page, promotes the activities of the Current Affairs Club from a critical stance: "A lack of interest in, and concern for, affairs of our state and nation would stand high on a list of criticisms of campus life at GSCW."

PG 67R "Hrump — not enough pride to build a nest!" *The Colonnade* (April 19, 1945): 4. This more conventionally styled political cartoon may have been inspired by O'Connor's study of *A Century of Political Cartoons* by Allan Nevins and Frank Weitenkampf (C. Scribner's Sons, 1944). The headline of an article published directly above her cartoon asks, "Must We Have Universal Military Service?"

PG 69L "Isn't it fortunate that Genevieve has completely escaped that boy-crazy stage?" *The Colonnade* (May 2, 1945): 4. While a student at GSCW, O'Connor regularly submitted her cartoons to *The New Yorker*. Cartoons like this one that appeared in *The Colonnade* during the final weeks of her senior year are unrelated to news copy or campus events, and may have been drawn from a portfolio of work created for submission elsewhere.

PG 69R "You don't mind if I get comfortable, do you?" *The Colonnade* (May 22, 1945): 4. This cartoon appears to revise a bit of W. C. Fields slapstick from *The Dentist*, a 1932 Mack Sennett Comedy. In the film's version of the joke, the dentist maneuvers himself between the patient's legs while drilling her teeth.

PG 71 "Yeah, I know it's a nice shoe, lady, but it's not exactly what I'm looking for." *The Colonnade* (June 6, 1945): 4. "Veterans Demand Normal Treatment," an article published side-by-side with O'Connor's cartoon, discusses war veterans reorienting to civilian life and their expectations upon returning to college: "The veteran may not want acceleration of study programs, but neither will he want unnecessary frills and delays."

The Alumnae Journal was published by GSCW's alumnae association. With the exception of the two cartoons in the Winter 1942 issue illustrating the article "Women Sailors!" about the arrival of the WAVES at GSCW, all of O'Connor's cartoons in this publication are reprints of popular cartoons from *The Colonnade*. In the Winter 1944 issue, the journal's editors included these words of praise for the school's "Cartoon Girl": "Again, the JOURNAL is delighted to present the work of GSC's gifted student-cartoonist, Mary

Flannery O'Connor, Milledgeville. Many of her cartoons, which appear originally in the student paper, the *Colonnade*, have already been run in the JOURNAL."

PG 73L *The Alumnae Journal* (Winter 1942): 3. The two original cartoons O'Connor submitted to *The Alumnae Journal* were illustrations for the article "Women Sailors!" The images dramatize the contrast between GSCW students at the turn of the century, shortly after the college was founded, and the new roles open to women. This cartoon portrays the GSCW student of an earlier time, as these lines from "Women Sailors!" described her: "Demure, circumspect, brown-serge-clad young ladies, mortar-boarded young ladies; collared-to-the-ears and skirted-to-terra-firma young ladies strolling academically down virgin college ways, Latin odes and a Gentlewoman's Choicest Formulae for Distinctive Viands and the simpler corollaries for Plane Geometry blending to form a gentle symphony so befitting an educational institution for the feminine of the species in the newly-turned century."

PG 73R *The Alumnae Journal* (Winter 1942): 3. This cartoon was the second illustration for "Women Sailors!" In contrast to the demure young ladies of the past, the WAVES were heralds of a modern era with more active roles for women. This cartoon provides an example of the "dozens and dozens and dozens of uniforms" described in "Women Sailors!" that soon would be seen on the GSCW campus, uniforms that were "not brown serge; not red-and-white striped shirtwaists; not academic gowns and oxford caps, but uniforms and a woman in each one of them...." The article described the change among young women at the college as shocking to Southern society.

The Corinthian, GSCW's student journal for creative writing and the arts, was published three times each year between 1942 and 1945. O'Connor worked on the journal's staff while a student at GSCW and regularly contributed art, poetry, essays, and stories to the publication. During her senior year, she served as the journal's editor.

PG 75L *The Corinthian* (Fall 1944): 12. These paired drawings were the first illustrations for O'Connor's essay "Fashion's Perfect Medium." The first figure, at the top, matches her description of the omnipresent baggy sweater: "Take sweaters for instance. By now they are practically standard. In fact, there are only two rules which govern their being worn – they must be either four sizes too large or three size too small – and since only those who weigh over two hundred and fifty pounds feel inclined to wear them three sizes too small, the oversize sweater is the only one to be considered."

The second figure in the set, below, represents a must-have in raingear, the reversible raincoat. O'Connor describes the correct etiquette for its use: "It is part of the unwritten law on all worthwhile campuses that no reversibles will be worn unless the inside lining is hanging down at least three inches below the outside. This holds true no matter which side is inside – whichever is, must hang."

PG 75R *The Corinthian* (Fall 1944): 13. The second pair of illustrations for O'Connor's essay on fashion continues the focus on sweaters, which were so long there appeared to be no need to wear a skirt. This trend will cause the skirt to "go out of existence or merge with the slip and one source of unconscious mental activity will be eliminated," or so O'Connor predicts.

The figure below represents the preoccupation with other feminine adornments, as O'Connor observes: "…some students decorate only with trinkets suggestive of a male donator in the armed services (this indicates that the wearer is not as repulsive as she may seem), others go to great pains to wear lengthy strands of pearls, knotted at some central point and hanging the rest of the way. This cuts the wearer exactly in half both diagonally and horizontally and undoubtedly takes great thought to execute."

PG 77L *The Corinthian* (Fall 1944): 14. An illustration for Joyce Moncrief's essay "You Can Have My Share" that ridicules the behavior of some GSCW students, this cartoon shows a girl arriving late to class, or almost. "Whoops, just made it!...No SIR! I had my foot an inch over the doorsill when that bell rang," Moncrief writes.

PG 77R *The Corinthian* (Fall 1944): 14. The second illustration for Moncrief's essay "You Can Have My Share" depicts the kind of student more prepared to make excuses than rush to class. "Wug! Gnkff?...You mean the bell rang ten MINutes ago? O'mahgawrsh! I'll be late to physics...YEP, That's it – I'll tell her I overslept," Moncrief writes.

PG 79L *The Corinthian* (Fall 1944): 15. The exaggerated features of the girl called "Glamourpuss" in Moncrief's essay "You Can Have My Share" are, apparently, the result of too much makeup. "Those eyes look like she must have run into a coupla doors in the dark, but confidentially – she puts that stuff on with a brush," Moncrief writes. And her lipstick?: "It's not a bad shade, although certain CATTY individuals might think it faintly reminiscent of that beet relish we sometimes have in the Dining Hall."

PG 79R *The Corinthian* (Fall 1944): 15. The final image for Moncrief's essay "You Can Have My Share" is a girl named "Tallulah," also known as the "girl with the hair-do" and "Her Royal Highness." A fashion snob with expensive taste, Tallulah "can't utter more than two sentences without dragging in the fact that she orders her garments from Foofnagles, Inc.," Moncrief explains. In O'Connor's cartoon, Tallulah is shown "heading down on that group of freshmen – with her copy of *Vogue*, of course," illustrating Moncrief's description.

The Spectrum, GSCW's yearbook, was published each spring. O'Connor worked on the yearbook staff in 1944. In 1945 she served as the yearbook's feature editor. In this role, she organized the yearbook as "A Pilgrimage through JESSIEVILLE…." Each section was a stop on the tour represented by a different O'Connor cartoon accompanied by a brief narrative.

PG 81 & 83L *The Spectrum* (1944): 74. These illustrations for the "Major Organizations" section of the yearbook, published with the following description, may represent caricatures of the students elected to lead these organizations: "Always there are leaders, whether older people or fellow students. On our campus, these are organized into three groups, our major organizations upon enrolling at G.S.C.W. We choose our leaders from among ourselves, and they represent us in College Government, Y.W.C.A, and the Recreation Association."

PG 83R & 85 *The Spectrum* (1944): 88. These illustrations for the "Publications" section of the yearbook, published with the following invitation, may represent caricatures of each publication's editor: "'Look into thy heart and write' for one of the three college publications – the *Corinthian*, the *Spectrum*, or the *Colonnade*. (Incidentally, it's the first step on the road to the madhouse.)"

PG 87 *The Spectrum* (1944): 96. O'Connor's satirical treatment of student activities continues with this scintillating depiction of a student meeting for the "Clubs" section of the yearbook. In the 1944 *Spectrum*, the artist receives the following note of praise from the editors: "Mary Flannery O'Connor, of cartoon fame, was the bright spot of our existence. There was always a smile in the *Spectrum* office on the days when her linoleum cuts came in."

PG 89L *The Spectrum* (1944): 127. For the 1944 *Spectrum*, the editors chose to present a chronicle of the year's events as recorded in the diary of a typical "Jessie," a common nickname for GSCW students. This cartoon illustrated that section of the yearbook, "The News and Views of Jessie Jones as Recorded in her Diary." Among her diary entries, Jessie Jones notes the origin of one of O'Connor's cartoons: "Friday, Feb. 25 – Election speeches before student body gave birth to M. F. O'Connor's next week's cartoon. 'I believe in students' rights, and if I'm elected fifth vice-president of, etc.…'"

PG 89R "This Is Jessieville," *The Spectrum* (1945): 4, 8. "Jessieville is not a myth, a place dreamed up in a fit of imagination. It's everything from the shady walks and columned porches to the music rooms and chemistry labs. Every building is a beloved, familiar landmark. It's the library, auditorium and Parks Hall...the books, brains and busyness these places house." This cartoon depicts the Old Governor's Mansion, a prominent campus landmark.

PG 91L "They Guide Us on Our Way," *The Spectrum* (1945): 4, 16. "Here are the ones who have traveled this way many times before and each time helping open new doors of learning and understanding for travelers like you and me. One can never forget a teacher of his favorite subject just as one can never stop appreciating his years spent in preparation, the books read, the travels made, the dollars spent, the kindliness and understanding, the spirit of seeking truth."

PG 91R "Wayfarers," *The Spectrum* (1945): 4, 28. "These are the travelers. Some are here for four years, some two and some only a few months. But each makes a footprint not easily erased. Remember when you first saw them... The upperclassmen, jaunty as though they felt so calmly sure they knew all the answers from Einstein to Ellington; the freshmen, sure of nothing except that they had lots to learn. Yes, lots to learn and lots to remember."

PG 93L "Our Naval Escort," *The Spectrum* (1945): 5, 78. "Some in our midst are dressed in Navy blue. They are just like the rest of us, only farther away from home, and sometimes more homesick, even though they proudly wear one of Uncle Sam's uniforms. Long after they're gone we'll still remember their cheerful singing as they march through the rain, the little short girl on the end of the platoon running to keep up, those jaunty salutes, their frequent and impressive graduations, and their smiling 'Hi' in reply to our 'Hey.'"

PG 93R "We Learn To Lead," *The Spectrum* (1945): 5, 82. "This past year we have learned more about living, and College Government, Young Women's Christian Association and Recreation Association have added greatly to the process. We've learned to lead, to be led, and to govern ourselves wisely. We've learned to look at the world and people about us with warmer hearts. We've learned to play and laugh and develop richer lives."

PG 95L "We Record Our Travels," *The Spectrum* (1945): 5, 96. "No journey is complete without a travelogue; so there are those who journey with us who chatter of copy and mutter of deadlines. These see stories in the daily routines and similes in each spring blossom. They are the ones who have inspired, informed and entertained us all along the way and now leave behind for travelers of other years a record of your year's pilgrimage."

PG 95R "Points of Interest," *The Spectrum* (1945): 5, 104. "Long after we have forgotten the date of the first barbarian invasion of Italy, we will still remember the endless practices for a College Theater play and the sudden blank memory as the first curtain rises. We can never forget the thrill of making one of the honoraries, or the excitement of band and choir trips. Clubs, committees, concerts make every day worth remembering."

PG 97L "Having a Wonderful Time," *The Spectrum* (1945): 5, 134. "We can count tomorrow and yesterday, and both of them are ours. This year we have counted each

month and preserved each bit and little event. Each yesterday has become a memory of a pleasant college association or experience that will rush back when one gets a letter from an old school friend, sees a student with a book, hears a familiar yell, or hears the voices of students softly singing the Alma Mater. We hold on to each yesterday and reach out to grasp our tomorrow."

PG 97R "Where Our Pennies Go," *The Spectrum* (1945): 5, 146. "From cokes to new radios, from a picture to send that Marine in the South Pacific to a new formal for the class dance, 'Jessies' are good consumers. So...our advertisers open wide their doors and we reply with 'Thank you.'"

Incidental artwork.

ENDPAPERS O'Connor's endpapers for the 1945 *Spectrum* offer a panoramic view of the GSCW campus populated with scenes familiar from her cartoons for the student newspaper, *The Colonnade*.

PG iv *The Corinthian* (Fall 1942): 9. O'Connor's staging originally provided an appropriately theatrical opening for Jane Sparks's essay "Sock and Buskin" about similarities in the dramatic arts from ancient to modern times.

PG 133 *The Corinthian* (Spring 1943): 6. This print served as an illustration for a poem by Mary Owens Salle, "I Like Fireflies Better Than Ants," and dominated the page above the poem. The poet finds one to be benevolent, beautiful, and illuminating, and the other a war-like, city-building busybody with a sting, as their insect expressions show.

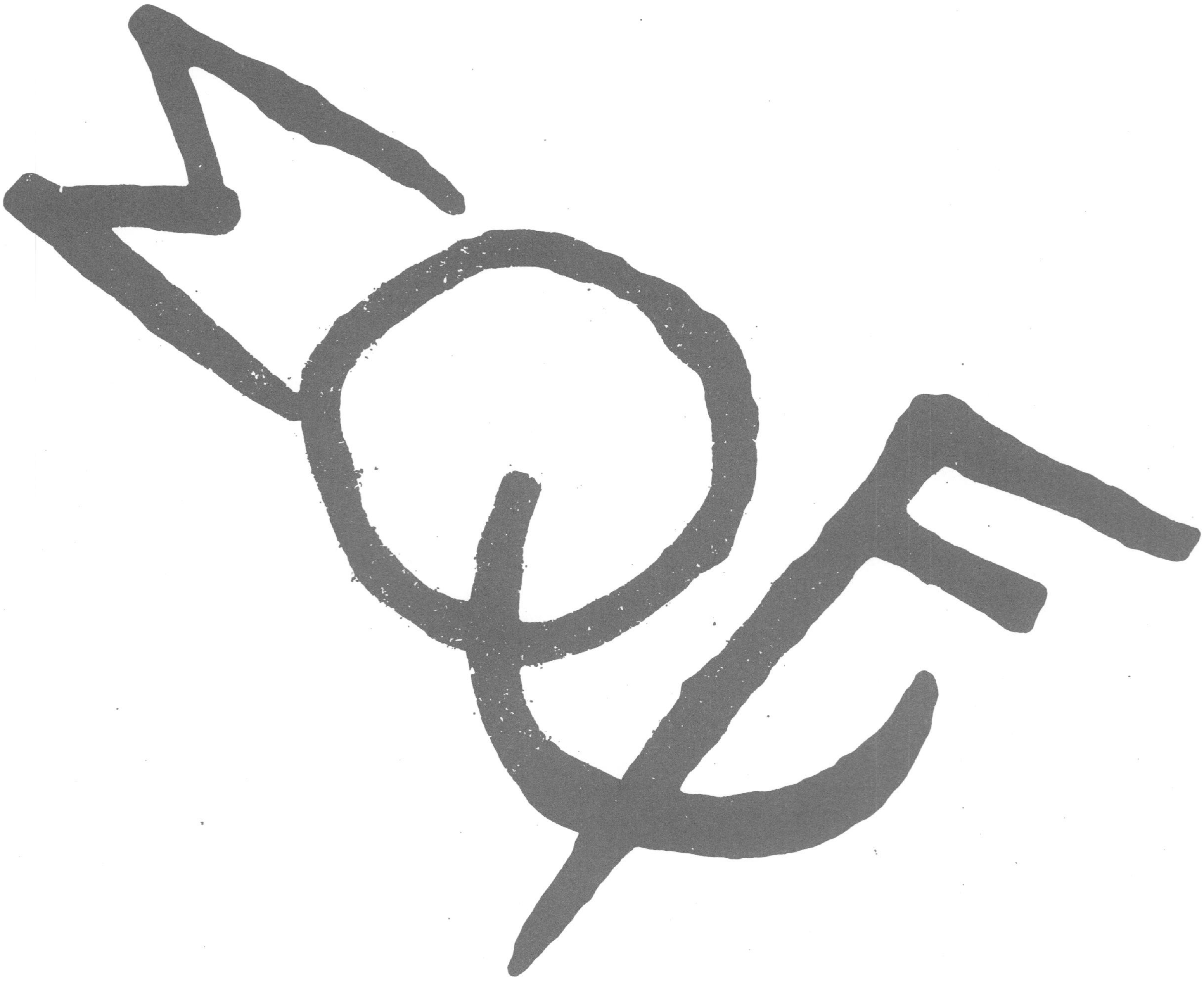